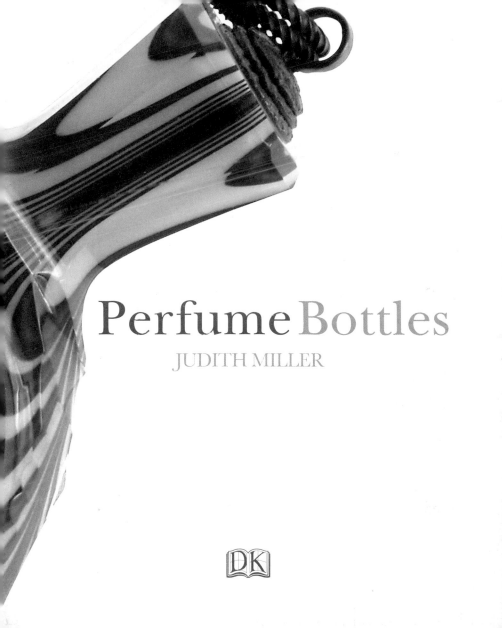

Perfume Bottles

JUDITH MILLER

DK

LONDON, NEW YORK,
MUNICH, MELBOURNE, DELHI

A joint production from DK and THE PRICE GUIDE COMPANY

DK DELHI
Designers Shefali Upadhyay, Kadambari Misra
Editors Aekta Jerath, Larissa Sayers
Cutouts Harish Aggarwal, Neeraj Aggarwal
Managing Art Editor Aparna Sharma

DK LONDON
Editor Katie John   Designers Lee Riches, Katie Eke
DTP, Reproduction, and Design Adam Walker
Production Elizabeth Warman
Managing Art Editor Heather McCarry

THE PRICE GUIDE COMPANY LIMITED
Publishing Manager Julie Brooke   Editor Jessica Bishop
Editorial Assistants Dan Dunlavey and Sandra Lange
Digital Image Co-ordinator Ellen Sinclair   Photographer Graham Rae

While every care has been taken in the compilation of this guide, neither the authors nor the publishers accept any liability for any financial or other loss incurred by reliance placed on the information contained in *Perfume Bottles*.

First published in the USA in 2006 by DK Publishing, Inc.
375 Hudson Street, New York, NY 10014

First published in Great Britain in 2006 by Dorling Kindersley Limited,
80 Strand, London WC2R 0RL
A Penguin Company

The Price Guide Company (UK) Ltd: info@thepriceguidecompany.com

2 4 6 8 10 9 7 5 3 1

CIP catalog records for this book are available from the Library of Congress and the British Library.

UK ISBN-13: 978 1 4053 0625 6
UK ISBN-10: 1 4053 0625 4

US ISBN-13: 978-0-7566-1922-0
US ISBN-10: 0-7566-1922-X

Proofing by MDP, UK
Printed in China by Hung Hing Offset Printing Company Ltd

Discover more at
www.dk.com

CONTENTS

4/5 07   2-12-09

INTRODUCTION

For thousands of years, the importance of perfume has led to the development of stunning and beautiful containers as varied as the scents themselves. These irresistible little works of art, from ornate Lalique flacons to funky Gaultier bottles, tell us so much about the era in which they were created it is no wonder they are widely collected today.

Once the domain of the wealthy, perfume is now an affordable luxury shared by millions of women around the globe. And a collection of perfume bottles can grow almost unintentionally – it is said that the average woman has more than six fragrances on her dressing table.

Judith Miller

Star Ratings

Each of the perfume bottles in this book has a star rating according to its value:

★ under $500; under £250 ★★ $500–1,000; £250–500 ★★★ $1,000–2,000; £500–1,000
★★★★ $2,000–4,000; £1,000–2,000 ★★★★★ $4,000 upward; £2,000 upward

PRE-20TH CENTURY

The Ancient Egyptians used aromatic substances In bathing, the Romans scented their banquet rooms with oils, and the Elizabethans steeped their clothes in fragrance to hide poor hygiene. Perfume has a long and fascinating history and the beautifully crafted bottles used to store it over the centuries demonstrate its importance. Perfume bottles were first used in 1000BCE, and since then, each has mirrored the latest tastes in fashion, technology, design, and art.

After falling out of fashion, with the decline of the Roman Empire, perfume was revived in the 16th century when scented pomanders became popular. Major perfume manufacturers such as Yardley were established in the 18th century and beautifully decorated bottles were produced. Improved manufacturing methods meant the 19th century saw a wealth of attractive bottles come onto the market, to hold gentle floral waters.

Roman unguentarium (ointment or cosmetic container) in blue glass. c.1st–3rd century CE ★☆☆☆☆

Roman unguentarium in honey-colored glass. *c.1st–3rd century CE*

☆☆☆☆
★

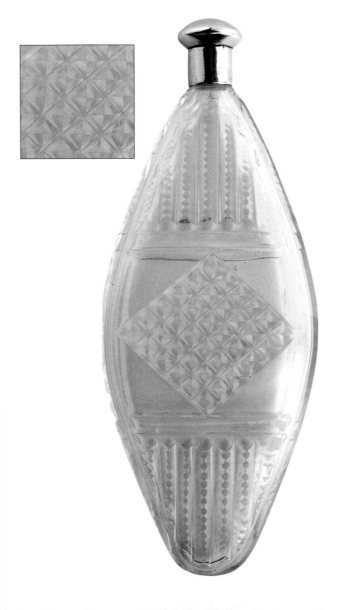

English clear glass perfume bottle,
in traditional ovoid shape.
Early 19th century ★ ☆☆☆☆

English clear glass perfume bottle with simple stopper and a silver top, probably made for a man.
Early 19th century ★★☆☆☆

Sandwich Glass paperweight perfume
bottle, in smoky canary yellow.
Mid-19th century
★ ★ ★ ★
☆ ☆ ☆

French Palais Royal turquoise opaline perfume bottle. *Mid-19th century* ★ ★ ★ ☆ ☆

Ruby cased glass perfume casket, with ormolu
mounts, two clear glass bottles, and key.
Mid-19th century   ★★★★☆

Ruby glass scent bottle with silver top. *19th century* ★☆☆☆

French perfume bottle, possibly Baccarat, with metal stopper and red and turquoise body. *Mid-19th century* ★★☆☆

COLORED GLASS

p.17

p.320

p.17

p.284

p.285

p.405

p.419

p.35

p.284

p.119

p.252

p.27

p.216

p.311

p.24

p.235

COLORED GLASS

Combined perfume bottle and vinaigrette by Samson Mordan, in emerald-green glass with engraved silver-gilt cap and base. *Mid-19th century* ★★☆☆☆

Dutch miniature perfume bottle, with raffia overlaid body and silver-gilt mounts.
Late 19th century ★ ☆ ☆ ☆

Scent bottle in cut red crystal over mercury, with hinged silver cover and stopper.
Late 19th century ★ ★ ★ ☆ ☆

English latticino blue and white perfume bottle, with pinchbeck stopper.
Late 19th century ★☆☆☆☆

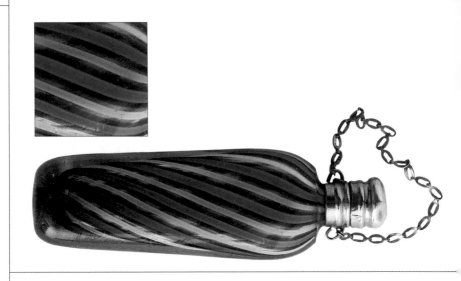

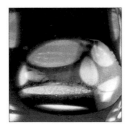

English clear glass perfume bottle, with blue overlay and silver top.
Late 19th century ★★☆☆☆

English white opaline cut-glass perfume bottle, with blue overlay and silver top. *Late 19th century* ★★ ☆☆☆

English smelling salts bottle with silver top. *Late 19th century* ★ ☆☆☆☆

English clear cut-glass perfume bottle, with blue enamel and silver top.
Late 19th century ★★☆☆☆

European agate perfume flask, with embossed silver-gilt hinged cap and stopper; probably Dutch. *Late 19th century* ★☆☆☆☆

European clear glass perfume bottle, with silver-gilt mount and faceted stopper; has original fitted case. *Late 19th century* ★★★☆☆

EARLY PERFUMES

Sweet oils and flower waters have long been used to mask smells and enhance attractiveness, but their use increased rapidly in the 18th century. King Louis XV of France ordered a different scent for his rooms every day, and Napoleon Bonaparte got through 60 bottles a month. Ordinary people mixed simple floral perfumes at home, while the wealthy commissioned their own perfumes. In addition, commercial firms appeared on the scene and increased the availability of scents such as lavender water.

During the 19th century, new technology and industrialization enabled goods to be produced on a greater scale and at a lower cost than ever before. From the 1870s, chemists experimented with synthetic oils, used in perfumes such as Houbigant's 1882 "Fougère Royale," that would make perfume an affordable luxury for more women.

English ruby glass perfume bottle, by G.E.W. Ltd., with cut decoration and screw cover. *Late 19th century* ★ ☆☆☆☆

European double-cased scent bottle, in pink and white cut crystal, with stopper and brass fittings. *Late 19th century* ★★☆☆☆

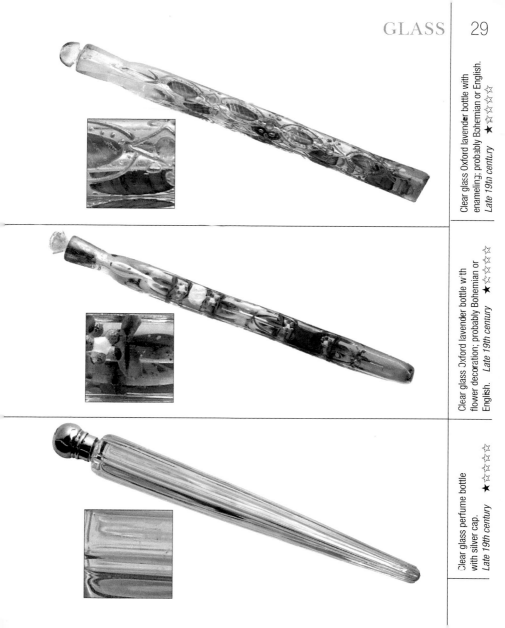

Clear glass Oxford lavender bottle with enameling; probably Bohemian or English. *Late 19th century* ★ ☆ ☆ ☆ ☆

Clear glass Oxford lavender bottle with flower decoration; probably Bohemian or English. *Late 19th century* ★ ☆ ☆ ☆ ☆

Clear glass perfume bottle with silver cap. *Late 19th century* ★ ☆ ☆ ☆ ☆

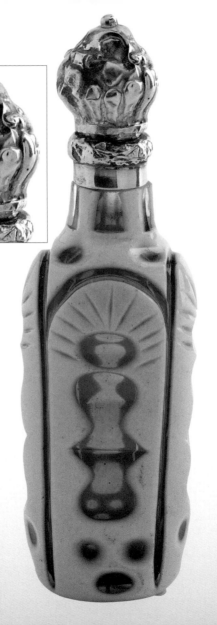

English cranberry glass perfume bottle with white enamel. *Late 19th century* ★★☆☆☆

French blue opaline scent bottle with round body and silver top
and chain.   *Late 19th century*   ★ ☆ ☆ ☆

VICTORIAN STYLE

Keeping up with the latest fashions was crucial to many Victorians. With more time on their hands and more money in their purses than people in earlier times, they could afford the luxury clothes, accessories, and perfumes necessary for making a good impression.

Perfume was purchased in plain packaging or disposable glass "Oxford lavenders" from the drug store, but was stored in highly decorative bottles, which reflected the fashions of that period. Toward the middle of the 19th century, designs became more ornate and cluttered. Silver bottles were heavily embossed, while ceramic examples were encrusted with flowers, and bright glass bottles were shaped with facets to catch the light. From the 1880s, the Aesthetic, Art Nouveau, and Arts and Crafts Movements made bottle shapes more graceful. At the same time, perfumers began to see the potential of commissioning bottles for specific fragrances.

Clear glass scent bottle with flower decoration and pinchbeck stopper. ★ ☆☆☆☆☆

English double-ended bottle in amber glass, with mirrored interior and embossed caps. *1870s* ★☆☆☆☆

English double-ended bottle in Bristol Blue glass, with brass mounts shaped like opera glasses. *1870s* ★★☆☆☆

English double-ended cranberry glass perfume bottle with faceted body and embossed caps. *1870s* ★ ☆☆☆☆

English double-ended scent bottle in ruby glass, divided for smelling salts and vinaigrette. *1870s* ★★ ☆☆☆

English clear glass double-ended bottle for perfume and salts, with ruby enamel and silver caps. *1880s* ★★☆☆☆

"A fragrance is like a signature, so that even after a woman leaves the room, her fragrance should reveal she's been there."

OSCAR DE LA RENTA

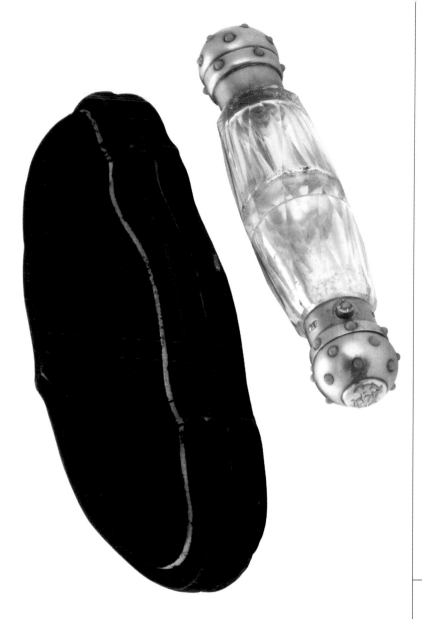

English clear glass double-ended perfume bottle with silver-gilt and coral mounts; also has fitted case. *1870s*   ★ ★ ☆ ☆ ☆

Double-ended perfume bottle with faceted body and chased silver-gilt caps. *1870s* ★ ☆☆☆☆

English double-ended perfume bottle in clear glass, with silver caps. *1880s* ★★☆☆☆

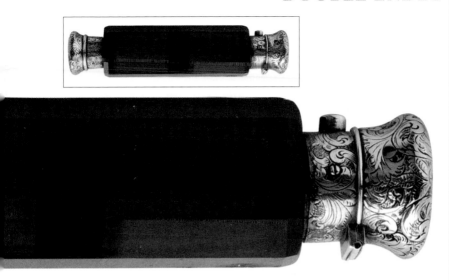

English red double-ended perfume bottle with two silver caps. *1880s*
★ ☆☆☆☆

English green double-ended perfume bottle with pinchbeck caps. *1880s*
★ ☆☆☆☆

Cobalt blue Bohemian perfume bottle overlaid in white. *1860s* ★☆☆☆☆

Unusual early Bohemian perfume bottle, with chinoiserie decoration and stopper resembling a reducing lens. *1840s* ★★★☆☆

Bohemian ruby flash engraved perfume bottle, with rare "umbrella" stopper. *19th century* ★★★☆☆

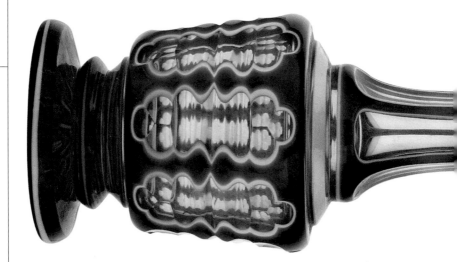

Bohemian double overlay perfume bottle. *1880s* ★★★☆☆

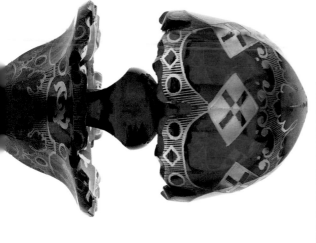

Gallé perfume bottle with cameo blossom and vine decoration in amethyst and blue, and matching amethyst stopper. *Late 19th century* ★★★☆☆

Gallé perfume bottle with purple cameo flowers; metal top has a pop-up atomizer pump. *Late 19th century* ★★★☆☆

Daum signed perfume bottle with acid-cut decoration of thistles, stems, and leaves; enamel gilt on thistles; and gilt border. ★ ★ ★ ☆ ☆

Stourbridge brilliant-cut cameo perfume bottle, with silver vermicular screw cap; probably by Stuart & Sons. Cap has London hallmark. *1987* ★ ★ ★ ★ ☆

English cameo perfume bottle with amethyst
and blue morning glory decoration and original
silver top.   *Late 19th century*   ★★★
★★★☆

Cranberry-tinted cameo bottle, decorated with trailing flowers and leaves. Embossed silver top has Birmingham mark. *Late 19th century* ★★☆☆☆

DETAIL: Characteristic decoration of applied flowers and shells.

POTTED HISTORY

Porcelain dinnerware by the great factories of Sèvres and Meissen was the height of good taste during the 18th and 19th centuries, and it was not long before fashionistas aspired to similar perfume bottles for their dressing tables. In the 18th century, Rococo bottles by English companies such as Chelsea were extremely popular. Bottles were usually adorned with applied flowers and leaves in pastels and gilt, or were occasionally painted with whimsical scenes. Rococo-style bottles were revived in the 19th century by companies such as Samson et Cie and Rockingham.

Wedgwood's Jasperware flasks, decorated in the Neo-Classical style, were also very desirable. Introduced in 1770, they were made from unglazed stoneware and decorated in white relief with Classical figures and garlands, inspired by cameo designs. Coalport, Spode, Royal Worcester, and various other makers also produced attractive ceramic perfume bottles, which are sought after today.

Spode perfume bottle and stopper, with applied flowers and shells on a pea green body.
Mid-1830s ★ ★ ☆ ☆ ☆

Chelsea porcelain perfume bottle with putto and dog. *18th century* ★★★★★

"A fragrance always combines femininity and sensuality."

GIANFRANCO FERRE

Pair of baluster-shaped Meissen perfume bottles, decorated with flowers; the stoppers have applied porcelain flowers. *c.1860* ★ ☆☆☆☆

Baluster-shaped Meissen perfume bottle, decorated with applied porcelain flowers. *c.1860* ★ ☆☆☆☆

Rare Rockingham bone china perfume
bottle, with applied flowers and gilded
foliage and rim. *1830s* ★★★☆☆

Rockingham china perfume bottle encrusted with flowers and foliage, and painted with gilt vines.   *1830s*   ★☆☆☆☆

"*A rose is a rose is a rose,
but a great perfume
creates emotion.*"
MICHAEL EDWARDS

Chamberlain Worcester porcelain perfume bottle with
gilt-metal mount and stopper. *1840s* ★★★☆☆

English glazed pottery perfume flask with screw cap, by Horton & Allday, Birmingham; imitation of Wedgwood Jasperware decoration. *1870s* ★☆☆☆☆

English mounted pottery perfume flask; fluted oval body is embellished with gilt flowers and a butterfly. *1880s* ★ ☆☆☆☆

Blue and white "Willow" pattern perfume flask; silver lid is marked "London 1886, Samson & Mordan." *1880s* ★ ☆☆☆☆

Porcelain perfume bottle with metal screw cap, and with hand-painted design of a couple in a landscape. *1890s* ★ ☆☆☆☆

☆☆☆
★ ★

Copeland Spode bone china perfume bottles, with gilt flowers, ironstone red paint, and silver screw covers by Samson Mordan of London. *1890s*

Brass scent bottle from Nepal, shaped like
an urn. *18th century* ★★☆☆☆

Rare silver perfume bottle from Amsterdam, shaped like a lute anc featuring a town scene. *18th century* ★★☆☆☆

Staffordshire enamel perfume bottle case, with
children and flowers on blue gingham background
and gilt highlights. *1770s*   ★★★★☆

Staffordshire enamel perfume bottle and bontonnière, decorated with scenes after Jean Antoine Watteau's paintings. *1770s* ★★★☆☆

Tortoiseshell and silver inlaid twin perfume bottle case. *Early 19th century* ★☆☆☆☆

French enamel gilded etui (ornamental case), inscribed "Sincer en amitie"; inside is a faceted glass bottle. *Mid-19th century* ★★★☆☆

French opaline cylindrical scent bottle or flacon in overlaid glass, with gothic-style brass stand. *1830s* ★★★☆☆

Black enamel on silver gilt perfume bottle showing Cupid and flowers, with hinged cover. *19th century* ★ ★ ☆ ☆

English novelty mounted glass perfume bottle and vinaigrette by S. Mordan & Co, shaped like a champagne bottle, with a simulated "foiled" neck and wired cap. 1870s ★★★★☆

> *"A scent can trigger spiritual, emotional, or physical peace and stimulate healing and wellness."*
> DONNA KARAN

Silver-gilt chatelaine with notebook, locket, perfume bottle, etter opener. and smelling-salts pot; this accessory would have been pinned to a lady's dress.   *1880s*   ★★★☆☆

METAL DECORATION

p.315

p.267

p.74

p.60

p.87

p.75

p.157

p.310

p.184

p.372

p.271

p.310

p.155

p.67

p.87

p.72

p.63

p.63

METAL DECORATION

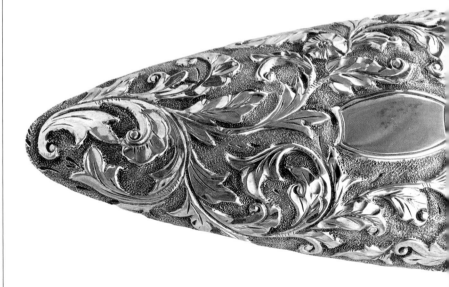

Drop-shaped perfume bottle, with stippled floral and bird decoration and screw top; has Birmingham marks. *1884* ★ ★ ☆ ☆

English perfume bottle in high relief silver, with maker's mark "SB&S." Hinged cover opens to show glass liner. *1880s* ★ ☆ ☆ ☆

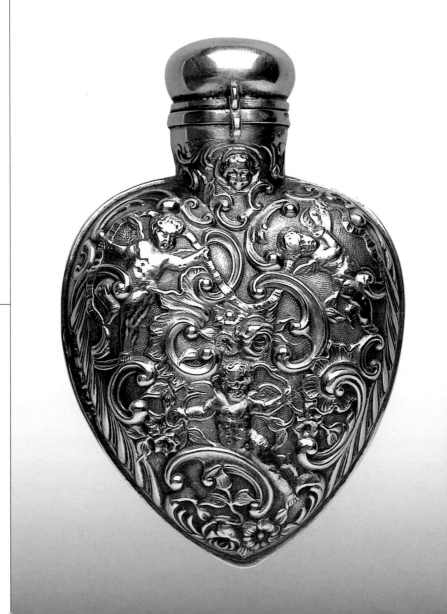

Silver perfume bottle with putto and rose decoration; has mark for William Comyns, London. *1898* ★★☆☆☆

English miniature silver perfume bottle case with stippled decoration. *1890s* ★ ☆ ☆ ☆

DETAIL Silver case opens to reveal tiny clear glass bottle.

English silver and glass perfume bottle, by Walter Thornhill of London. *1890s* ★★★★★

METAL & ENAMEL

Russian silver and cloisonné enamel perfume
bottle, with maker's marks "BK" and "84."
Late 19th century
★★★ ☆☆

Russian cloisonné enamel perfume flask, decorated in blues and foiled reds, by unascribed maker with marks for Moscow. *Late 19th century* ★★☆☆☆

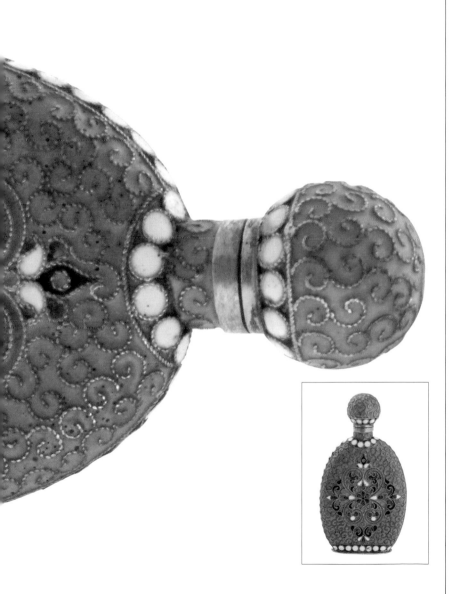

DETAIL: Hinged grille, pierced and engraved with foliage.

VINAIGRETTES

The practice of carrying vinaigrettes, tiny containers for aromatic vinegars, developed from the use of the pomander. In the Middle Ages, "pomander" balls of scents and spices were stashed in silver cases and carried to disguise bad personal hygiene. These containers gradually became more decorative. By the 18th century, the vinaigrette had arrived on the market. A tiny sponge soaked in scented vinegar was placed inside the case and covered with an ornate pierced grill so that it could be inhaled to mask bad odors. The interior was usually gilded to prevent corrosion. Typical examples are heavily engraved or embossed, and are small enough to be carried in the palm of the hand, tucked into a lady's glove. Vinaigrettes were often incorporated into scent and smelling-salt containers, and double-ended bottles were a popular choice.

Small Viennese enamel vinaigrette, with design depicting courting couples. *1870s* ★★★ ☆☆

English silver vinaigrette with engraved foliate design and gilt interior, and with hallmark for E. Smith of Birmingham. ★ ★ ☆ ☆ ☆

Silver vinaigrette by Lea & Co., shaped as articulated fish and engraved with fins and gills. *Early 19th century* ★ ★ ☆ ☆ ☆

Silver-gilt vinaigrette with fine barley-pattern sides and heavy scrolling borders.   1824   ★★★☆☆

Silver vinaigrette with two ornate initials on the cartouche, and with hallmark for D&F.   *1897*   ★ ★ ☆ ☆ ☆

Vinaigrette by Thomas Brough of London, with foliage design on exterior. *Early 19th century* ★☆☆☆☆

DETAIL: Gilt interior, with pierced grille.

Silver vinaigrette by Yapp & Woodward, with a lake scene engraved on lid, and with intricately carved grille. *1840s* ★★★☆☆

"What remains of a woman when she is in the dark?
When she has undressed, when we can no longer see her
make-up, her wonderful hair; her beautiful eyes, when
she's taken off her jewelry, what is left?
Only her charming voice and her perfume."

JEAN-PAUL GUERLAIN

PRESENTATION BOTTLES

Gold and cornelian shaped flat scent bottle, with
original chain.   *18th century*   ☆☆
★★★

Dutch perfume flask, carved from a Coquilla nut.
Late 18th century ★★☆☆☆

Palais Royal domed casket, containing three opaline perfume bottles.
Mid-19th century ★★★★☆

PRESENTATION BOTTLES

Tunbridgeware coromandel pin cushion and
scent bottle stand, with tesserae bands of flowers.
19th century ★ ★ ☆ ☆

VICTORIANA

p.20

p.40

p.58

p.35

p.21

p.34

p.71

p.98

p.25

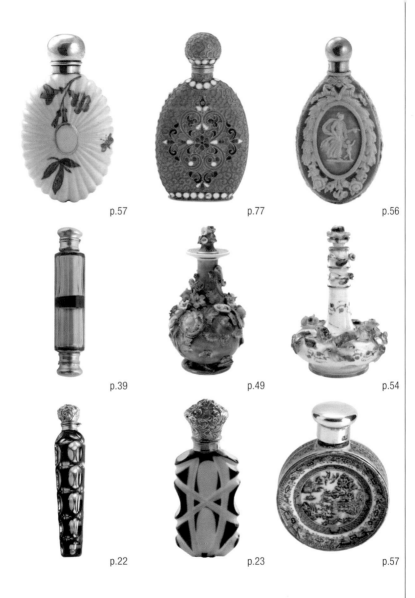

p.57

p.77

p.56

p.39

p.49

p.54

p.22

p.23

p.57

VICTORIANA

English "peddler" doll. Her tiny basket contains miniature perfume bottles and a pair of scissors. ★★★ ★★☆☆

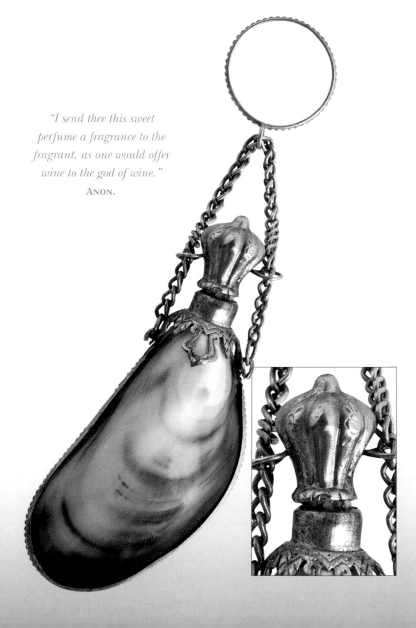

"I send thee this sweet perfume a fragrance to the fragrant, as one would offer wine to the god of wine."

ANON.

Perfume bottle formed from two shells, with pinchbeck stopper, chain, and ring.
Mid–late 19th century ★ ☆ ☆ ☆

Mauchline ware twin perfume bottle case
with Chapelle du Chateau scene on lid.
19th century ★☆☆☆☆

Two perfume bottles, with original stoppers, made
by Baccarat. *19th century* ★ ☆☆☆☆

European ebony and tortoiseshell perfume bottle box, with brass fittings. *19th century*

★★★☆☆

PRESENTATION BOTTLES

English coromandel and gilt-brass casket, containing cut-glass bottles with silver gilt mounts. *1872* ★★☆☆☆

EARLY 20TH CENTURY

The first two decades of the 20th century saw the beginning of the modern world as we know it. Women won the right to vote, the US movie industry was established, Kellogg's started selling cornflakes, and the Model T Ford was famously released in "any color as long as it's black." New production techniques meant perfume, and the bottles it was sold in, could be produced on a grander scale than ever before. Woman could now buy attractively packaged brand name perfumes over the counter from makers such as Pinaud and Dralle.

The fresh, feminine style of the "La Belle Epoque" banished heavy Victorian fashions to the past and, a few years later, the Art Nouveau movement, with its swirling organic forms, took the design world by storm. To stand out on the shelf, commercial bottles were produced in the new styles and became more decorative.

Baccarat "La Rose de Gabilla" perfume bottle for Gabilla, in original box. ★★☆☆☆

Baccarat "Le Parfum D'Antan" perfume bottle, in clear and frosted crystal, with box. ★★★★☆

Baccarat "Le Secret de Dieux" perfume
bottle, for Yardley, with recessed gilt
detail.

★★★★ ☆

Baccarat "Toujours Fidèle" perfume bottle for D'Orsay, in clear and frosted crystal, with box. ★★☆☆☆

Baccarat "Moda" perfume bottle for Gabilla, in clear crystal with recessed and enamel detail. ★★★★☆

p.151

p.114

p.264

p.102

p.137

p.111

p.294

p.120

p.130

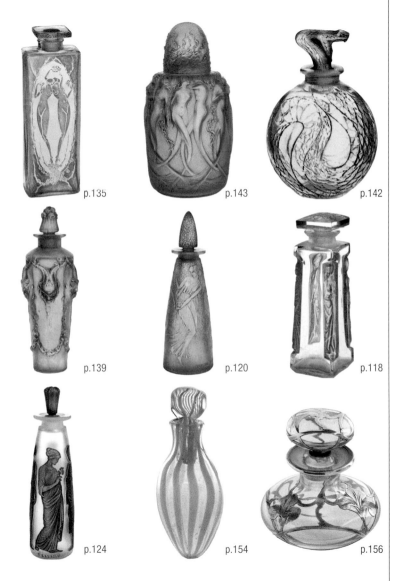

p.135

p.143

p.142

p.139

p.120

p.118

p.124

p.154

p.156

ART NOUVEAU STYLE

Baccarat "La Vierge Folle" perfume bottle for Gabilla of Paris. ★★☆☆☆

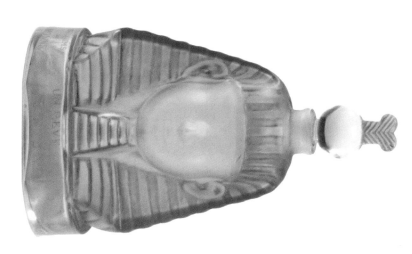

Baccarat "Ramses IV" perfume bottle, shaped as a sphinx. ★★★★★

☆ ★★★ ★★

Baccarat "Parfum des Champs-Elysées"
perfume bottle for Guerlain, in crystal, with box.

Cristallerie De Paris "Parfum Precieuse" bottle for Caron, in opal and white crystal with leather box. ★★★★☆

"Perfume is an art form, in the same genre as music and painting. It requires talent, expertise, and most of all passion."

CLIVE CHRISTIAN

Depinoix "Bouquet de Papillons" bottle for Lubin, in clear and frosted glass. ★ ★ ☆ ☆

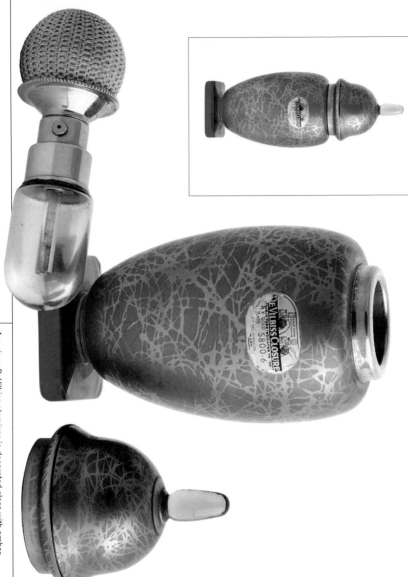

American DeVilbiss atomizer, in decorated glass with amber glass foot and finial. ★★☆☆☆

German Dralle "Illusion" perfume bottle, with box and papers, packaged in wooden case.

☆☆☆☆
★

Millefiori, Italian for "one thousand flowers," is a form of glass made from fused slices of glass canes.

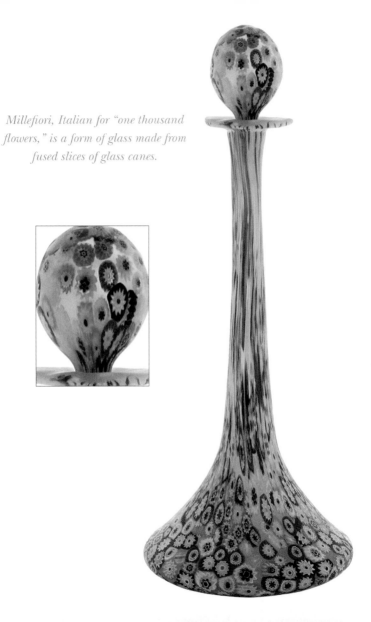

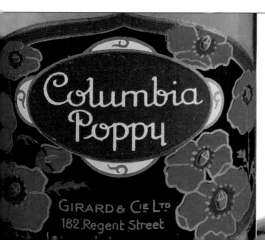

Girard & Cie. "Columbia Poppy" perfume bottle, with paper label, fabric seal, and card box. ★ ★ ☆ ☆ ☆

LALIQUE

Few great names in the world of 20th-century glass cause as much excitement as that of Lalique, the leading French glassmaker. René Lalique (1860–1945) opened his first glass shop in Paris in 1905, and started to produce finely crafted bottles for Coty. Innovative techniques allowed his beautiful designs to be mass-produced at a low cost and to a high standard, which enabled him to attract clients such as D'Orsay, Houbigant, and Roger et Gallet. Lalique's Art Nouveau pieces typically feature floral and figural etched designs and are extremely valuable.

The Art Deco period saw the company build on earlier successes. Shapes were bold and sometimes featured over-sized decorative stoppers. An original box can greatly increase the value of these bottles. Over the years, Lalique produced thousands of bottles for more than 60 perfume manufacturers, and it is still in business today.

Lalique "Le Lys" perfume bottle for D'Orsay, in clear and frosted glass with sepia patina. ★ ★ ☆ ☆ ☆

Lalique "Ambre" perfume bottle for D'Orsay, in clear and frosted glass with sepia patina. ★★★☆☆

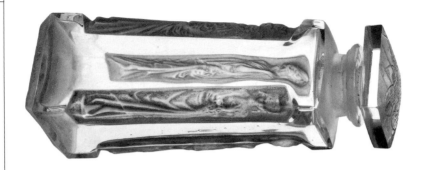

Lalique "Ambre" perfume bottle for D'Orsay, in clear and frosted glass with blue patina. ★★★☆☆

Lalique "Ambre" perfume bottle for D'Orsay, in black glass with white patina. ★★★☆☆

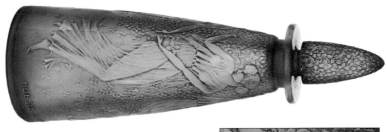

Lalique "Poesie" perfume bottle for D'Orsay, in clear and frosted glass with sepia patina. ★★★★☆

Lalique "L'Elegance" perfume bottle for D'Orsay, in clear and frosted glass with sepia patina. ★★★★☆

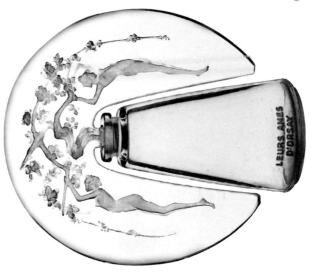

Lalique "Leurs Ames" perfume bottle for D'Orsay, in clear and frosted glass with sepia patina. ★★★★

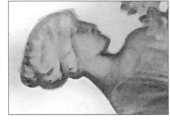

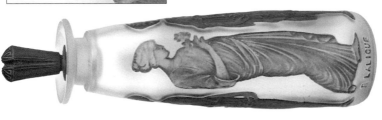

Lalique "Ambre Antique" perfume bottle for Coty, in frosted glass with sepia patina. ★★★☆☆

FIGURES & FACES

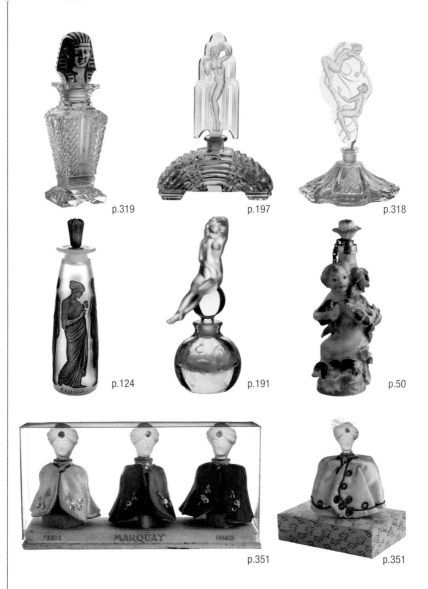

p.319

p.197

p.318

p.124

p.191

p.50

p.351

p.351

p.94

p.178

p.163

p.361

p.147

p.239

p.291

p.338

Lalique "L'Effleurt" perfume bottle for Coty, in clear and frosted glass. ★★★★★

Lalique "Ambre Antique" perfume bottle for Coty, in frosted glass with gray patina. ★★★☆☆

Lalique "Mystère" perfume bottle for D Orsay, in black glass. ★★☆☆☆

Lalique perfume sample tester box for Coty, in wood and bronze, with 12 glass bottles by Depinoix. Plaque inside lid is signed "R. Lalique." ★★★★★

Lalique "L'Effleurt" perfume bottle for Coty, in clear and frosted glass with gray patina. ★★★★

"A perfume needs to attract the eye as much as the nose."

FRANÇOIS COTY

Lalique "Styx" perfume bottle for Coty, in clear and frosted glass with sepia patina. ★★☆☆

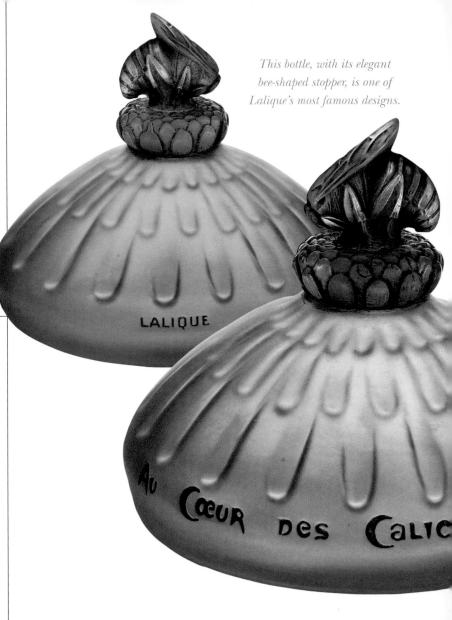

This bottle, with its elegant bee-shaped stopper, is one of Lalique's most famous designs.

Lalique "Au Coeur des Calices" perfume bottle for Coty, in blue glass with gray patina.

★★★★★

COTY

LALIQUE

Lalique "Flausa" perfume bottle for Roger et Gallet, in clear and frosted glass with sepia patina. ★★★★☆

"A fragrance is like a cat burglar
in your brain; it has the key with which to pick the
lock and unleash your memories."

ROJA DOVE, FRAGRANCE EXPERT

Lalique "Quatre Cigales" perfume bottle, in clear and frosted glass with blue patina. ★★★★☆

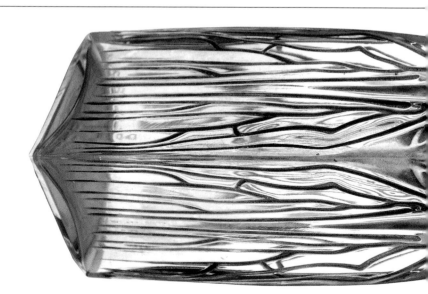

Lalique "Quatre Cigales" perfume bottle, in clear and frosted glass with gray patina. ★ ★ ★ ☆ ☆

Lalique "Panier de Roses" perfume bottle, in clear and frosted glass with blue patina. ★★★★☆

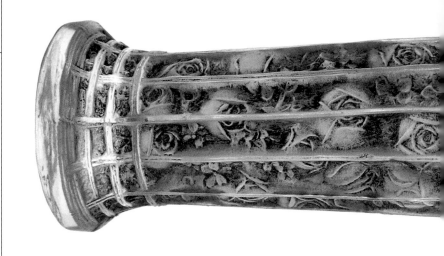

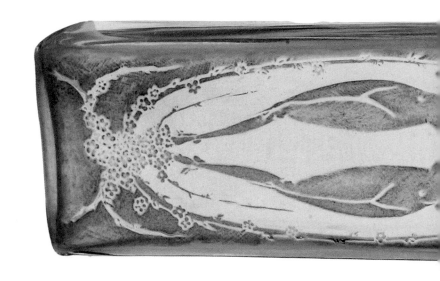

Lalique "Lepage" perfume bottle, in clear and frosted glass with green patina. ☆★★ ★★★

Lalique's fine craftsmanship is evident in this stopper. The willowy nudes with their flowing hair are typical of the Art Nouveau style.

Lalique "Deux Figurines, Bouchon Figurines" perfume bottle, in clear and frosted glass with sepia patina. ★★★★★

Lalique "Rosace Figurines" perfume bottle, in clear and frosted glass with sepia patina. ★★★★☆

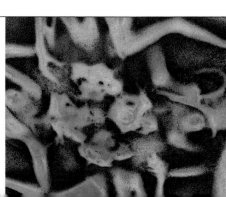

Lalique "Pan" perfume bottle, in clear and frosted glass with sepia patina. ★★★ ☆☆

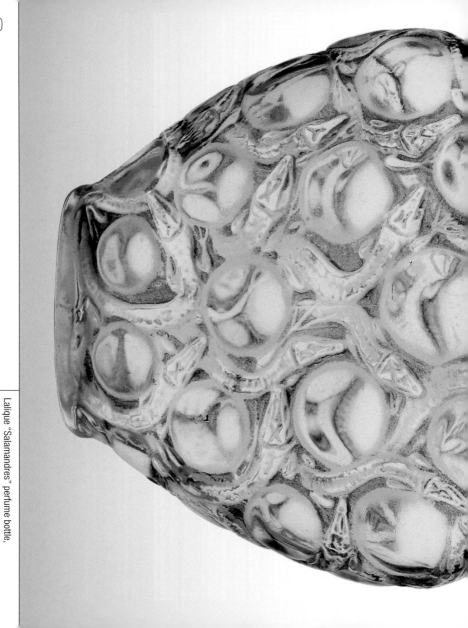

Lalique "Salamandres" perfume bottle, in clear and frosted glass with blue patina. ★★★★☆

> *"To create a perfume you have
> to be the servant of the unconscious.
> Each idea evolves and transforms,
> but there should be a surprise
> with each note."*
>
> **SERGE LUTENS, PERFUMER**

Lalique "Serpent" perfume bottle, in clear and frosted glass with gray patina.
★★★★☆

Lalique "Sirènes" perfume burner, in clear and frosted glass with blue patina. ★★★☆

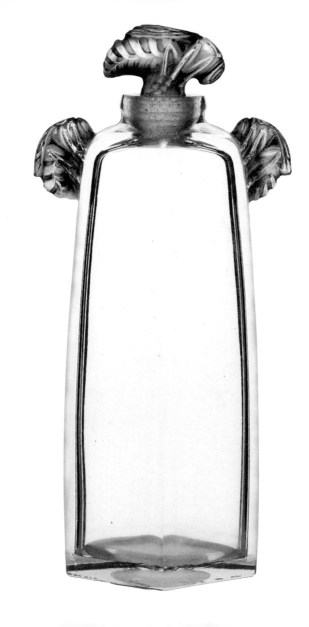

★★
★★★☆

Lalique "Trois Guêpes" perfume bottle, in clear and frosted glass with gray patina.

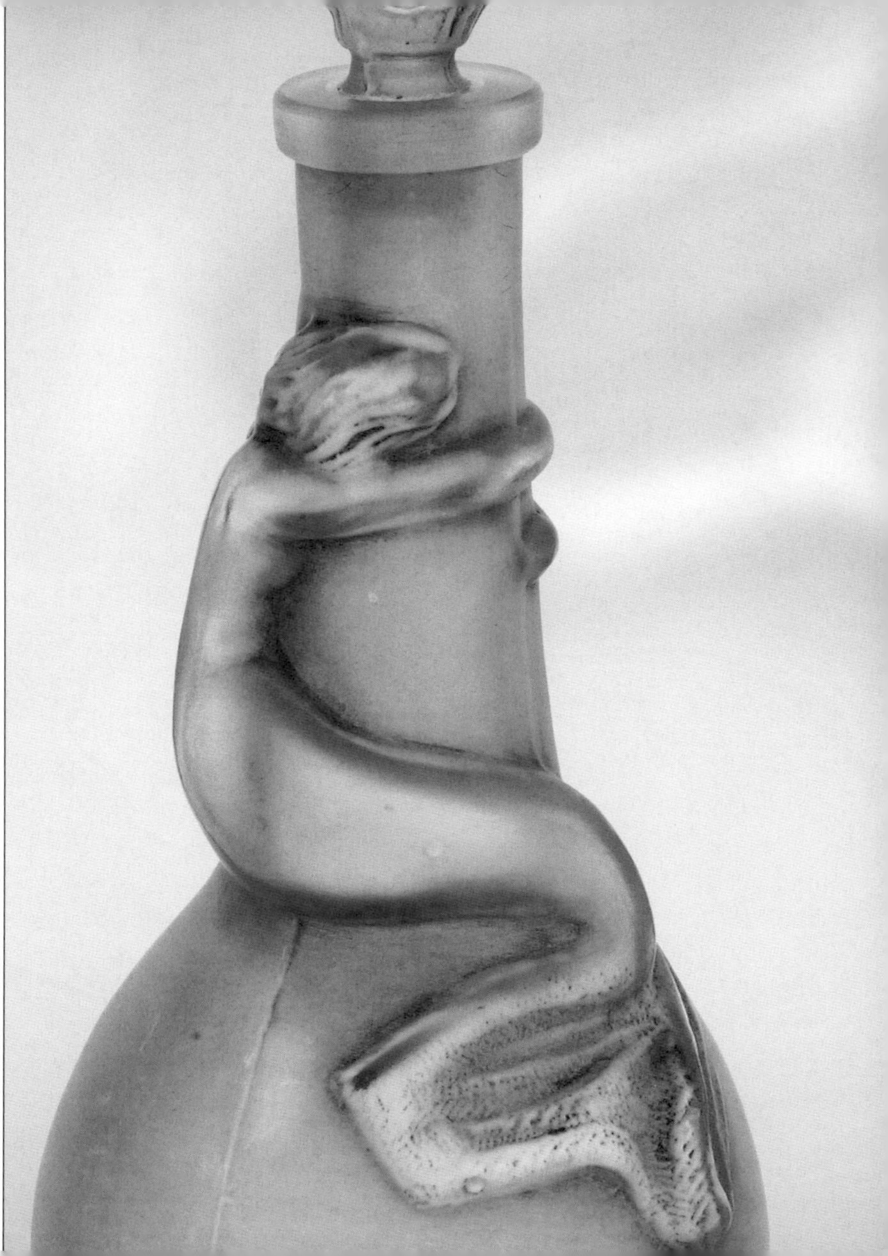

ART NOUVEAU

Willowy nudes, organic shapes, and sinuous flowers: the 1890s saw a revolution in design. The Art Nouveau movement, which lasted until the start of the First World War, turned away from the heavily ornate forms of the previous era and embraced fresh and modern designs. The new look could be seen everywhere, from Hector Guimard's Parisian Métro entrances to Charles Rennie Mackintosh's Scottish Willow Tea Rooms. It influenced all sorts of commercial products, from furniture to advertisements, and perfume bottles were no exception. High-end perfumers such as Coty, Roger et Gallet, and D'Orsay commissioned

great glassmakers such as Lalique and Baccarat to produce beautiful bottles in the new style, while more ordinary containers were finished with attractive labels featuring Art Nouveau decoration. Early 20th-century bottles with strong Art Nouveau styling are very valuable today.

Perfume bottle by Lefebure & Cie. glassworks, in frosted glass with sepia stain. ★★★☆☆

Parfumerie Oriza "Depose" bottle, labeled "Violettes, Prince Albert." ★ ☆☆☆☆

AN EXPLOSION OF BRANDS

The modern perfume industry emerged during the early 20th century, when a huge number of new commercial manufacturers sprang up. Keen to entice customers, companies produced ever more eye-catching packaging. Instead of buying perfume in plain packaging to decant into decorative containers at home, women started looking for scents that were sold in appealing bottles.

The "art glass" trend inspired glass forms and decoration by makers such as Lalique and Baccarat, and even labels were bright and attractive. DeVilbiss offered the first atomizer bottle, using a mechanism initially invented by the company's founder, Dr. Allen DeVilbiss, in 1887 to help treat throat conditions. French perfumers such as D'Orsay, Pinaud, and Roger et Gallet competed with British firms such as Dubarry and German ones such as Dralle. This variety ensures that commercial bottles from the period remain popular.

Parfymeri F. Pauli of Stockholm "Extrait des Fleurs" perfume bottle, with original box. ★☆☆☆☆

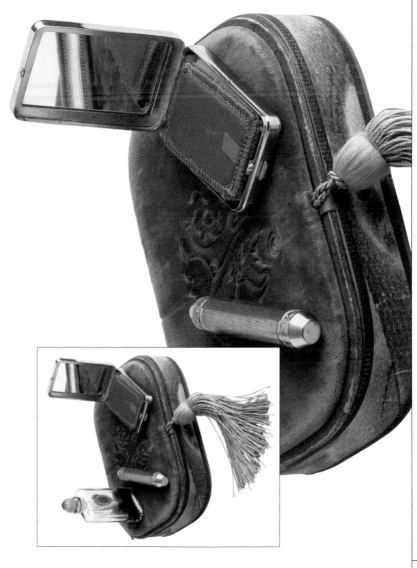

Richard Hudnut "DuBarry" gift set,
comprising perfume bottle, compact, and
lipstick ★★☆☆☆

Latticino glass (from the Italian for "small, milk-white") is traditionally made from clear and white glass rods twisted together to make stripes.

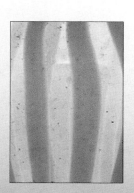

English latticino clear and white perfume bottle with glass stopper. ★☆☆☆☆

The top of the cap is embellished with rose-cut diamonds and has a violet-hued amethyst at the center.

Belle Epoque cut crystal perfume bottle with gold cap. ★★★★

★ ☆☆☆☆

Clear glass perfume bottle, probably German.

European silver perfume bottle case, inset with red glass eyes, with import marks for London. ★ ☆ ☆ ☆ ☆

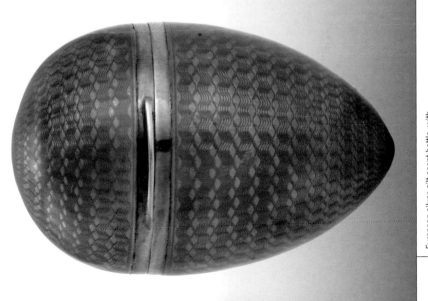

European silver-gilt scent bottle, with translucent enamel on an engine-turned ground. ★ ★ ☆ ☆ ☆

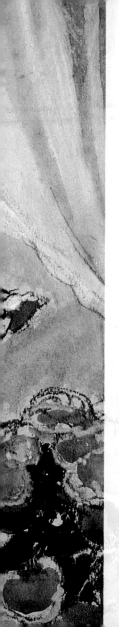

1920s–1930s

The Roaring Twenties, The Jazz Age, Art Deco: whatever you associate with the period after WWI, it's impossible to ignore the excitement, elegance, and innovation of the era. It seemed that the world had broken with the recent past irreconcilably. Women were enjoying greater freedoms than ever before, abandoning their corsets, lifting their hemlines, and making-up their faces. The Gibson girl, the American ideal of the 1900s, had been replaced with the glamorous, drinking and dancing flapper. As wearing fragrance became more fashionable, the perfume industry grew rapidly. Fashion legends, such as Coco Chanel, Schiaparelli, and Jean Patou, launched their own designer scents and large manufacturers competed with each other by introducing ever more innovative packaging. Making use of modern materials such as Bakelite, as well as more traditional crystal, bottle shapes were influenced by radical movements in the arts including Cubism, Surrealism, and modernist architecture.

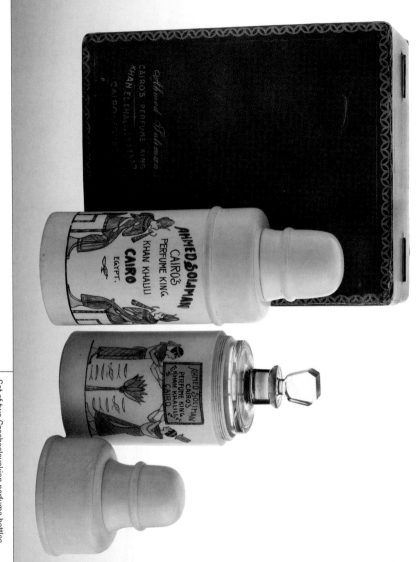

Set of two Czechoslovakian perfume bottles for Ahmed Soliman, with dauber stoppers and faux ivory cases. *1930s* ★★★★☆

★ ★ ★ ☆ ☆

Babani "Giardini" perfume bottle, ir green glass
with gilt and enamel detail. *1920s*

Large Baccarat "Mitsouko" perfume bottle for Guerlain, in clear crystal with label. *1930s* ★★★☆☆

Baccarat "Toquade" perfume bottle for Silka, in clear and frosted crystal with recessed name labels. *1920s* ★★★☆☆

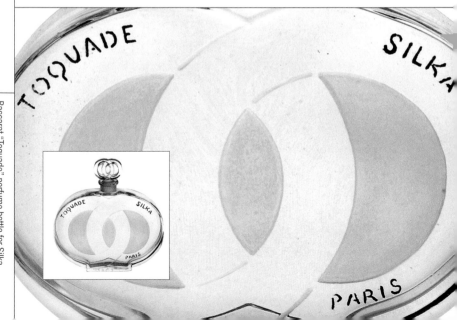

Baccarat "Ming Toy" figural perfume bottle for Forest, in
clear crystal with enamel details.   *1920s*   ★★★ ★☆

Baccarat "Le Dandy" perfume bottle for D'Orsay, in black crystal with label and original box. *1920s* ★ ☆ ☆ ☆ ☆

Baccarat "It's You" perfume bottle for
Elizabeth Arden, in white crystal with enamel
and gilt details. *1930s* ★★★☆☆

CYCLAMEN

BACCARAT

Many of the greatest luxury perfumes of the last century were supplied in stunning bottles made by glass manufacturer Baccarat. Established in 1764 in France, the company soon managed to attract the attention of Parisian perfume houses, such as Guerlain and Pinaud, with its exquisite flacons. Early commercial examples were fairly plain in design, but by the turn of the century, Baccarat was competing with Lalique by producing ornate bottles in the fashionable Art Nouveau style.

Always able to adapt to the latest tastes, the company employed sculptor George Chevalier in the 1920s and began producing bottles inspired by the Art Deco movement. During the 1930s, Schiaparelli and Elizabeth Arden topped the client list and experimental bottle shapes were influenced by Surrealist art. The golden age of Baccarat perfume bottles came to an end with the start of the Second World War, although bottles continued to be produced for high-profile perfumers after this time.

Baccarat "Cyclamen" perfume bottle for Elizabeth Arden, in white and clear crystal with gold detail. *1930s* ★★★★☆

Baccarat "It's You" perfume bottle for Elizabeth Arden, in clear and frosted crystal with enamel ring, on display stand. ★★☆☆☆

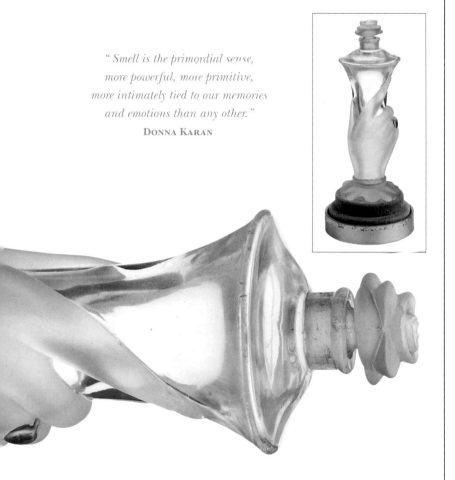

" *Smell is the primordial sense,*
more powerful, more primitive,
more intimately tied to our memories
and emotions than any other. "
DONNA KARAN

Bourjois "Evening in Paris" perfume bottle, with Bakelite stopper. *1930s* ★☆☆☆☆

Bourjois "Miss Kate" perfume bottle by
Saint-Louis, in clear and black crystal, with
label ard box. *1920s* ★★★☆☆

BOURJOIS

Prior to the "naughty nineties" – the 1890s – make-up was frowned on by respectable women. However, the last years of the 19th century saw a radical change in fashions. Bourjois, founded in 1869 to produce make-up for actresses, capitalized on the new interest in cosmetics. Dry rouge and powder blush, sold in the little round pots that remain a company trademark today, were soon on the market.

In 1928, the perfume "Evening in Paris", one of the company's most successful products, was launched. As well as the lure of the fragrance, the innovative and appealing packaging was key to its success. The blue and silver bottle was designed by Jean Helleu and evoked the glamor and sophistication of a Parisian evening. Other significant perfumes by the company include "Etoile D'Amour," "Kobako," and "Miss Kate."

Bourjois "Evening in Paris" blue glass perfume bottle, with novelty Eiffel Tower presentation. *1928* ★ ★ ☆ ☆

Bourjois "Kobako" perfume bottle by Borsse, with Bakelite box and stand. *1930s* ★★☆☆☆

DETAIL: Decorative case, made from Bakelite, with peony design.

Bourjois "Evening in Paris" owl perfume bottle case, in blue Bakelite. *1920s* ★☆☆☆☆

DETAIL: Hinged front of case opened to reveal glass perfume bottle.

Breyenne "Chu Chin Chow" perfume bottle, in blue and opaque white glass, with gilt and enamel detail. *1920s* ★★★☆☆

Rare Breyenne "Heure Exquise" perfume bottle, in blue glass with gilt detail, and with velvet cushion box. *1920s* ★★★★ ☆

Trio of Cardinal perfumes, "Bouquet," "Chypre," and "Gardenia," in "Tantalux"-inspired presentation. *1930s* ★☆☆☆☆

Caron "Les Pois de Senteur de Chez Moi" perfume bottle. *1920s* ★ ☆☆☆☆

Caron "Le Narcisse Noir" perfume bottle, with black glass flower stopper and box. *1911* ★ ☆☆☆☆

CHANEL

The history of 20th-century fashion would have been very different without the unmistakable designs of Coco Chanel (1883–1971). Classic clothing, as well as her understated accessories, earned her the devotion of women enjoying the new-found freedoms of the 1920s.

In 1922, Chanel launched a revolutionary new perfume. Comprising synthetic substances as well as natural extracts, the fragrance was a huge contrast to the floral perfumes that flooded the market at the time. The perfume was named Chanel No.5, supposedly because it was the fifth sample offered to the designer by the great perfumer Ernest Beaux. It became an instant success, as it enabled women who could not aspire to a designer suit to own a piece of affordable Chanel luxury. Like Coco Chanel's other designs, the bottle was simple and chic, and it remains largely unchanged today.

Chanel No.5 perfume bottle. This classic perfume remains popular even today. *1922* ★ ☆ ☆ ☆ ☆

Cherigan "Chance" perfume bottle, in opaque blue glass, with applied glass horseshoe and silver-gilt stopper. *1920s* ★★☆☆☆

Coty "L'Aimant" perfume bottle, with box, introduced in 1927.
★ ☆ ☆ ☆ ☆

BOHEMIAN GLASS

Ruby reds, rich golds, and deep blues: the area of Eastern Europe once known as Bohemia has long been famed for its exciting, opulent glass. By the 19th century, Bohemian glassmakers were able to produce bright, bold pieces that suited the tastes of the expanding middle classes, as well as being within their budget. Pieces were sometimes etched, and a popular technique was "flashing," whereby clear glass was thinly coated with amber, red, or violet glass and fired.

Bohemian glass briefly fell out of fashion during the Art Nouveau period, but after the First World War, glass from the newly named Czechoslovakia enjoyed a revival. Czechoslovakian glassmakers embraced the Art Deco movement during the 1920s and 30s, and produced bold, striking pieces that were popular throughout the world.

Czechoslovakian perfume bottle in amber crystal and metalwork set with blue jewels and pearls. *1920s* ★ ★ ☆ ☆ ☆

Czechoslovakian perfume bottle in amber crystal. *1930s* ★★☆☆☆

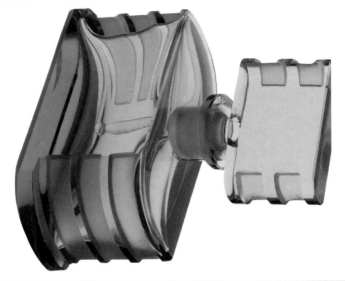

Czechoslovakian perfume bottle in blue crystal, with silver paper label. *1930s* ★★☆☆☆

Czechoslovakian perfume bottle, in green crystal and metalwork set with blue and green jewels. *1920s* ★ ★ ☆ ☆ ☆

Czechoslovakian perfume bottle in purple crystal, with enamel and jeweled metalwork. *1920s* ★ ★ ☆ ☆ ☆

Czechoslovakian perfume bottle in amber crystal, with clear and frosted stopper and metalwork set with enamel and jewels. *1920s* ★★☆☆☆

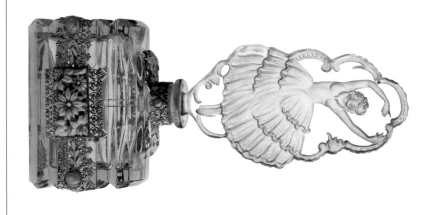

Czechoslovakian perfume bottle in blue crystal and metalwork set with enamel and jewels. *1920s* ★★☆☆☆

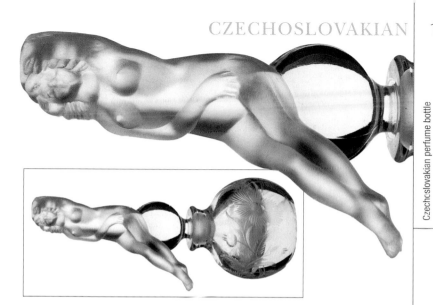

Czechoslovakian perfume bottle in clear, frosted, and engraved crystal. *1930s* ★★☆☆☆

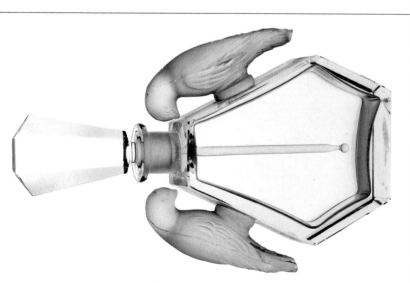

Czechoslovakian perfume bottle in clear crystal, with applied model birds. *1920s* ★★☆☆☆

Czechoslovakian perfume bottle for Ahmed Soliman, in marbled, purple-cased crystal with gold detail. *1930s* ★★☆☆☆

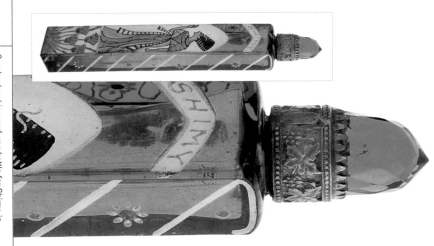

Czechoslovakian perfume bottle for Shimy, in green crystal with enamel details and jeweled filigree metal cap. *1930s* ★★☆☆☆

Czechoslovakian Art Deco bottle with atomizer. *1920s* ★★☆☆

Czechoslovakian Art Deco perfume bottle. *1920s* ★★☆☆

BOHEMIAN STYLE

p.190

p.187

p.222

p.217

p.223

p.41

p.42

p.42

p.192

p.226

p.188

p.189

p.219

p.228

p.189

p.216

BOHEMIAN STYLE

Weil "Antilope" perfume bottle, with engraved "W" on stopper. *1930s* ★ ☆ ☆ ☆ ☆

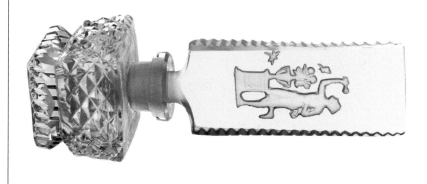

Amber cut glass perfume bottle, with clear glass stopper featuring two herons. *1930s* ★ ★ ☆ ☆ ☆

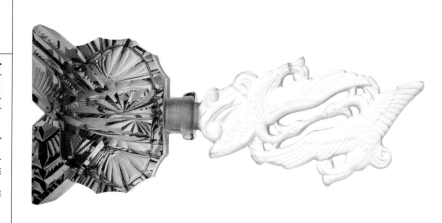

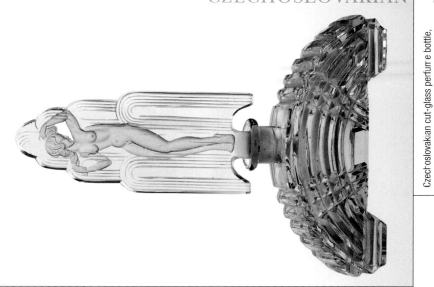

Czechoslovakian cut-glass perfume bottle, the stopper etched with a nude female figure *1930s* ★ ★ ☆ ☆

Large Czechoslovakian cut-glass perfume bottle, with cut-out stopper. *1930s* ★ ☆ ☆ ☆

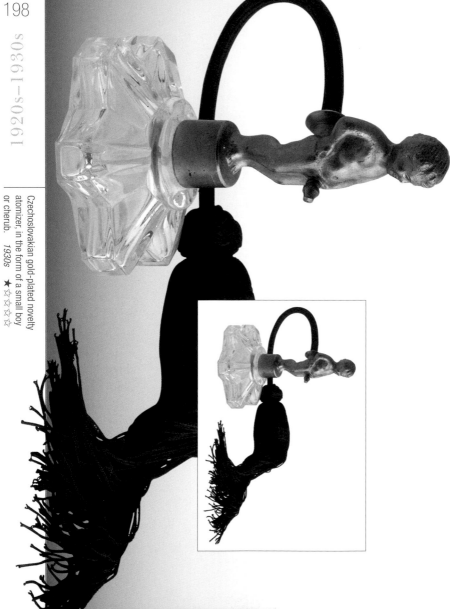

Czechoslovakian gold-plated novelty atomizer, in the form of a small boy or cherub. *1930s* ★☆☆☆☆

Czechoslovakian Art Deco perfume atomizer, in cut crystal with blue carved enamel decoration. *1930s* ★ ☆ ☆ ☆ ☆

D'Orsay "Trophee" miniature perfume bottle, in crystal with a label.   *1930s*   ★★☆☆☆

Depinoix "Kai Sang" perfume bottle for Corday, in black glass with enamel detail. *1920s* ★★★☆☆

The base of the bottle has an embossed label reading "Les Fontaines Parfumées, Grasse."

Depinoix perfume bottle for Pelissier-Aragon, in clear and frosted glass with sepia stain and enamel. *1920s* ★★★★☆

Depinoix "Lune de Miel" perfume bottle for Sari, in opaque black glass with silver-gilt detail and label. *1920s* ★★★☆☆

Depinoix "Hattie Carnegie" perfume bottle for Hattie Carnegie, in black glass with gilt details. *1920s* ★★★★☆

Depinoix "Contes Choisis" perfume bottle for Marcel Guerlain, in clear and frosted glass with sepia stain and label. *1920s* ★★☆☆

Set of two Celui by Jean Dessès perfume bottles, with red leather case. *1930s* ★ ☆☆☆☆

POWER BY DESIGN

During the early 20th century, competition between perfume-makers intensified and companies began to experiment with increasingly elaborate bottles in order to turn heads at the perfume counter. Since the late 19th century, perfume manufacturers had recognized the importance of attractive packaging, but it was not until the 1920s that its potential as a marketing tool was fully realized. Hugely different tactics were tried; bottles were either fashionable and sophisticated or surreal and attention-grabbing. Viard introduced beautifully designed bottles in glamorous boxes, Ota's "Bouquet" came in tiny pearl bottles, and DeVilbiss created ornate daubers and atomizers for applying perfumes. Each bottle by almost every maker was a tiny work of art.

The wealth of exciting packaging made from the 1920s through to the 1950s, and by contemporary makers such as Jean-Paul Gaultier, have made 20th-century perfume bottles a popular collecting area.

DeVilbiss Imperial perfume bottle with dauber, set with faux jewels in metal filigree. *1920s* ★★★★★

DUBARRY

Richard Hudnut "Dubarry" boxed set, with perfume bottle, compact, and lipstick.   *1920s*   ★ ☆☆☆☆☆

ELIZABETH ARDEN

Elizabeth Arden "Carnation" miniature perfume
bottle in opaque green glass, with flower inside;
has clear-fronted box. *1930s*
★★ ☆☆
★★★

Fragonard set of perfume solids, "Supreme," "5,"
and "Xmas," in wooden barrel containers with
presentation box. *1920s* ★☆☆☆☆

Lucien Gaillard "Pourpre d'Automne" perfume bottle for Violet, in clear glass with painted flower details. *1920s* ★ ★ ☆ ☆ ☆

1960s–1930s

"I think allure is something around you, like a perfume or like a scent. It's like a memory ... it pervades."

DIANA VREELAND

Gilot Perfume "Cajolerie" perfume bottle, with original box. *1930s* ★☆☆☆☆

Early Guerlain "Liu" perfume bottle, in clear glass with stopper; introduced in 1926. ★☆☆☆☆

DETAIL: Label showing trade mark.

Guerlain "L'Heure Bleue" perfume bottle; originally introduced in 1912. ★ ☆ ☆ ☆

Guerlain "No.90" perfume bottle. "No.90" was the temporary name of the famous "Shalimar" perfume. ★ ☆ ☆ ☆

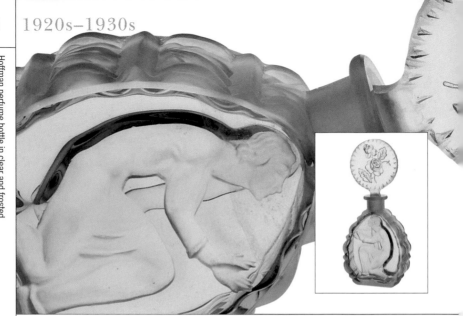

Hoffman perfume bottle in clear and frosted green crystal. *1920s* ★★☆☆☆

Hoffman perfume bottle in vaseline crystal. Its pale yellow-green hue is created by the inclusion of uranium. *1920s* ★★★☆☆

Hoffman perfume bottle in clear and frosted crystal. *1920s* ★★☆☆☆

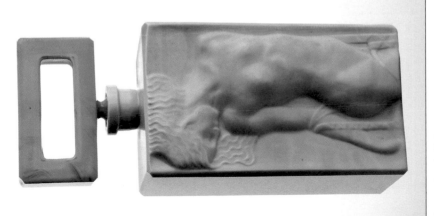

Hoffman perfume bottle in opaque turquoise crystal. *1920s* ★★★★★

HOFFMAN & INGRID

Master craftsman Heinrich Hoffman (1875–1939) was responsible for some of the most striking Czechoslovakian perfume bottles of the 20th century. Working from an atelier in Paris, he put his bold, ornate designs into production in Eastern Europe. Early examples show Art Nouveau influence, while 1920s and 30s pieces are distinctly Art Deco. Geometric shapes, Classical motifs and oversized stoppers are recurrent themes. Hoffman also contributed to the glassmaking ventures of his son-in-law Henry Schlevogt (1904–84), which resulted in the beautiful "Ingrid" range of bottles. These pieces typically feature complex agate, marble, and stone finishes and often have nude or opaque daubers. Occasionally, bottles had Austrian brass mounts, sometimes enhanced with carved stone or glass cabochons.

Hoffman perfume bottle, in pink crystal, mounted with jewels and a miniature ivory portrait. *1920s* ★★★☆☆

Hoffman perfume bottle in opaque black crystal with pale yellow stopper. *1920s* ★★☆☆☆

Hoffman perfume bottle in black and opaque green crystal. *1920s* ★★★★★

Hoffman perfume bottle in opaque black
crystal with green crystal plaque of St. George
slaying a dragon. *1920s* ★★★☆

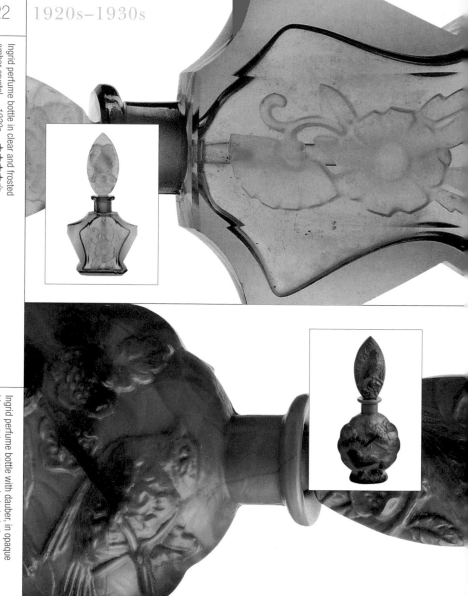

Ingrid perfume bottle in clear and frosted amber crystal.   *1920s*   ★★★★☆

Ingrid perfume bottle with dauber, in opaque blue crystal.   *1920s*   ★★★★☆

*The "Ingrid" range of bottles was named
after their creator Heinrich Hoffman's
grand-daughter.*

Ingrid perfume bottle in clear crystal with
opaque red stopper.   1930s   ★ ★ ☆ ☆ ☆

ART DECO STYLE

p.269

p.188

p.309

p.309

p.207

p.315

p.308

p.293

p.308

p.222

p.245

p.191

p.307

p.197

p.193

p.258

p.253

The clear stopper is embellished with a frosted flower design.

Ingrid perfume bottle in opaque blue crystal and metalwork set with Bakelite rose jewels. *1920s* ★★★☆☆

Ingrid perfume bottle in opaque black crystal, with frosted flower stopper and dauber. *1920s* ★★★☆☆

Ingrid perfume bottle in opaque green crystal, with clear and frosted stopper. *1920s* ★★★☆☆

"Some of the most beautiful perfumes are like a ballgown, but sometimes, you just want to wear a comfortable pair of jeans."

CHRISTOPHER BROSIUS

☆☆☆☆☆ ★

Jago & Jerome "Worthington Pale Ale" perfume bottle, containing "Jasmine" perfume. *1930s*

DETAIL: Stylized " JP" logo of manufacturer.

JEAN PATOU

Advertising a new fragrance as "the most expensive perfume in the world" was a bold move, but it seemed to pay off for couturier Jean Patou. Famous for his sporty and Cubist creations, the designer had decided in 1925 to follow in the footsteps of fellow couturiers Coco Chanel and Paul Poiret by launching three perfumes: "Amour Amour," "Que sais-je," and "Adieu Sagesse." Although these scents were popular at the time, it was the best-selling "Joy" that was to establish Jean Patou's name as a perfumer.

Initially only available to Patou's couture customers, "Joy" was introduced to the public in 1930, to add a touch of glamor to women's lives during the Depression. The perfume contained over 100 different ingredients and lived up to its slogan.

The bottle for his 1935 "Normandie" perfume, made to commemorate the launch of the famous ocean liner of the same name, featured a replica of the ship and is especially sought-after today.

Jean Patou "Joy" perfume bottle, in clear glass with a gold label; originally launched in 1930. ★ ★ ☆ ☆ ☆

Jean Patou "Joy" perfume bottle, with gold label and gold card box. ★☆☆☆☆

Two Jean Patou "Joy" perfume display bottles, in black with red stoppers. ★★☆☆☆

These bottles are influenced by Oriental style and resemble 19th-century snuff bottles.

Jean Patou "Moment Suprême" miniature perfume bottle, with bcx. *1930s* ★ ☆☆☆☆

Lalique "Marquita" perfume bottle, in blue glass. *1920s* ★★★☆☆

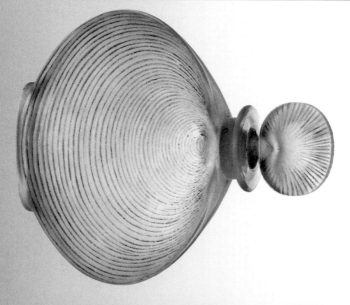

Lalique "Telline" perfume bottle, in clear and frosted glass with blue patina. *1920s* ★★★☆☆

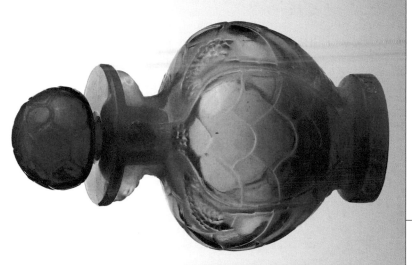

Lalique "Morabito No.7" perfume bottle, in cased yellow amber glass. *1920s* ★ ★ ★ ☆

Lalique "Amelie" perfume bottle, in clear and frosted glass with sepia patina. *1920s* ★ ★ ☆ ☆

Lalique "Le Parisien" atomizer for Molinard, in clear and frosted glass with sepia patina and gilt metal. *1920s* ★★★☆☆

"A fragrance always combines femininity and sensuality."

GIANFRANCO FERRE

Lalique "Calendal" atomizer for Molinard, in clear and frosted glass with sepia patina, and with gilt metal top. ★★★☆☆

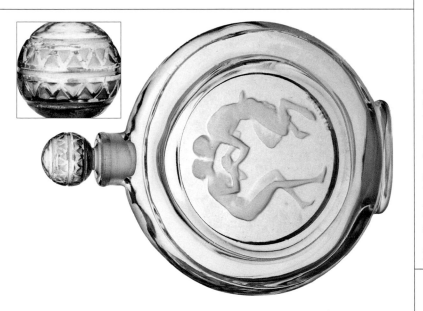

Lalique "Le Baiser du Faune" perfume bottle for Molinard, in clear and frosted glass, with leather display case. *1920s* ★★★★

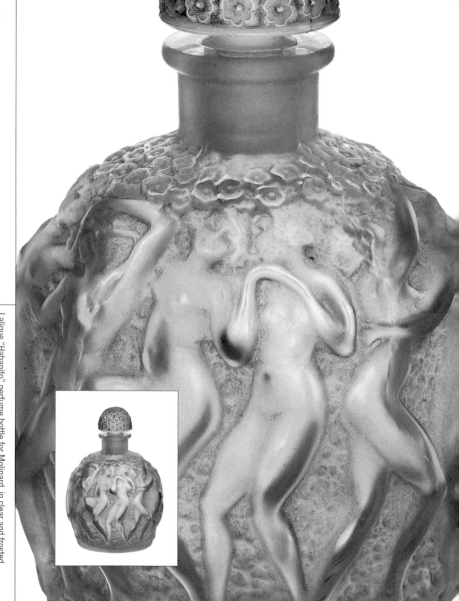

Lalique "Habanito" perfume bottle for Molinard, in clear and frosted glass with green patina. *1920s* ★★★★☆

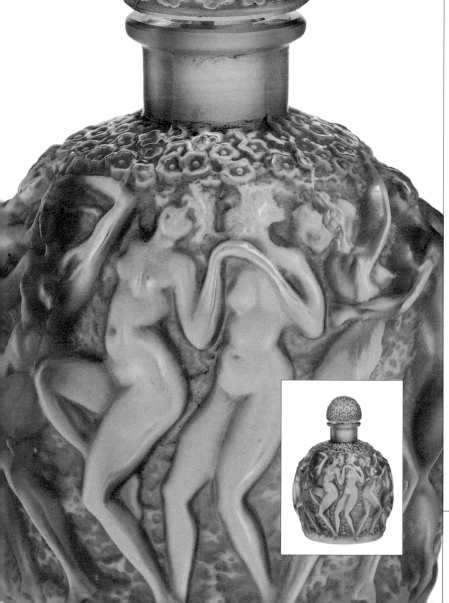

Lalique "Habanito" perfume bottle for Molinard, with sepia patina. *1920s* ★★★☆

Mona
Lisa
MADE IN FRANCE

THE ART OF GLASS

The craze for beautifully designed glass, intended for display rather than use, became widespread during the late 19th century as makers started focusing on high-quality materials, design, and craftsmanship. Among the most innovative glass artists was Emile Gallé (1846–1904), who is best known for his spectacular cameo glass. During the early 20th century, Daum, Steuben, and Venetian makers attracted a great deal of attention, and at the same time, the glorious vases and lamps of Tiffany were causing a stir all over the world.

Lalique, Baccarat, and other glassmakers took the same approach, emphasizing quality and good design to create stunning glass that was both attractive and useful. The techniques and decoration used by the great glass artists has influenced the designs of perfume bottles over the years, with many bottles, such as Schiaparelli's "Shocking" and Bourjois' "Evening in Paris," becoming design classics.

Lalique 'La Phalène' perfume bottle for D'Heraud, in deep amber glass. ★★★★★

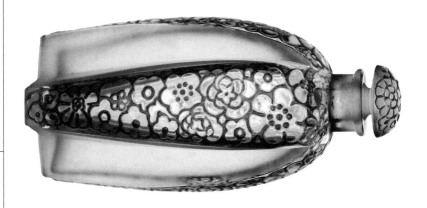

Lalique "Toutes les Fleurs" perfume bottle for Gabilla, in clear and frosted glass with red patina. *1920s* ★★☆☆☆

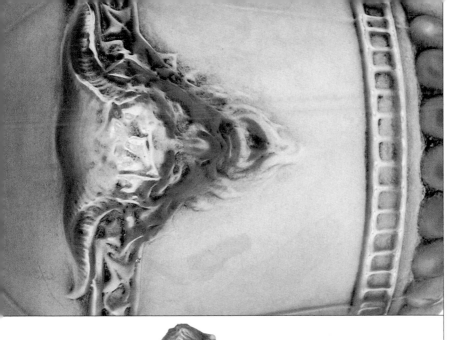

Lalique "Bouquet de Faunes" perfume bottle for Guerlain, in clear and frosted glass with gray patina. *1920s* ★★☆☆☆

Lalique "Dans la Nuit" perfume bottle for Worth, in clear glass with blue enamel. *1920s* ★★☆☆☆

Lalique "Sans Adieu" perfume bottle for Worth, in green glass, on a chrome and wood stand. *1920s* ★★☆☆☆

Lalique "Je Reviens" perfume bottle for Worth, in blue glass with chromed metal case. *1920s* ★★☆☆☆

Lalique "Danaë" perfume bottle for Magasin du Louvre, Paris, in clear and frosted glass with sepia patina. *1930s* ★★★☆☆

Lalique "Figurines No.1" atomizer for Marcas et Bardel, in glass with blue patina and gilt metal. *1920s* ★★☆☆☆

Lalique "Le Parfum des Anges" perfume bottle for Oviatt, in clear and frosted glass with sepia patina. ★★☆☆

LALIQUE CHIC

p.250

p.241

p.134

p.237

p.242

p.412

p.127

p.423

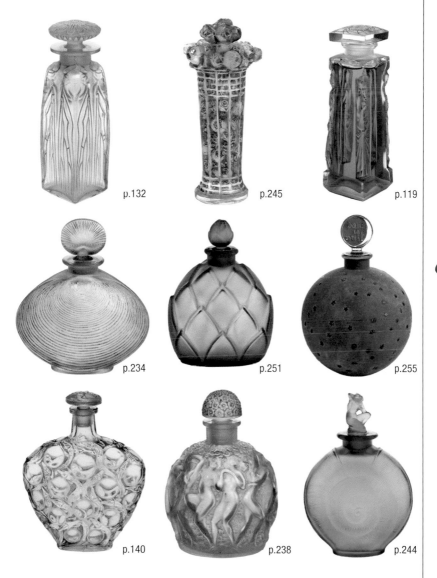

p.132

p.245

p.119

p.234

p.251

p.255

p.140

p.238

p.244

LALIQUE CHIC

Lalique "Le Jade" perfume bottle for Roger et Gallet, in green glass, with silk box and decorative tassel.
★★★★★

Lalique "Pavots d'Argent" perfume bottle for Roger et Gallet, in clear glass, with card box. *1920s*
★★★☆☆

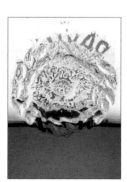

"I believe a fragrance should make you feel more yourself."

MASSIMO FERRAGAMO

Lalique opalescent glass atomizer, with relief design of nudes and with brass hardware. ★ ☆ ☆ ☆

Lalique "Amphitrite" perfume bottle, in green glass. *1920s* ★ ★ ★ ★

Lalique "Amphitrite" perfume bottle, in clear and frosted glass with blue patina. *1920s* ★★★★☆

Lalique "Camille" perfume bottle, in blue glass. *1920s* ★★★☆☆

Lalique "La Belle Saison" perfume bottle for Houbigant, in clear and frosted glass with sepia patina. *1920s* ★★★☆☆

Lalique "Myosotis Flacon No.3" perfume bottle, in clear and frosted glass with green patina. *1920s* ★★★★★

*"Nothing is more memorable than a smell.
One scent can be unexpected, momentary,
and fleeting, yet conjure up a childhood
summer beside a lake in the mountains."*

DIANE ACKERMAN, WRITER

Lentheric "Au Fil de L'Eau" perfume bottle in clear and green glass, with tasseled box. *1920s* ★★☆☆☆

Rare Lentheric of Paris "Tweed" perfume bottle, in clear glass with stopper. *1930s* ★☆☆☆☆

☆☆☆☆ ★
Lionceau "La Saison des Fleurs" presentation set of perfume
solids, in novelty Bakelite containers.   *1930s*

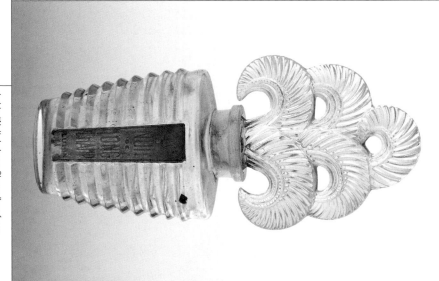

Lubin "Nuit de Long Champ" perfume bottle, with bold firework design to stopper. *1930s* ★☆☆☆☆

Lucien Lelong "Indiscrete"
perfume bott e, with bow-shaped
stop er. *1930s* ★ ☆☆☆☆

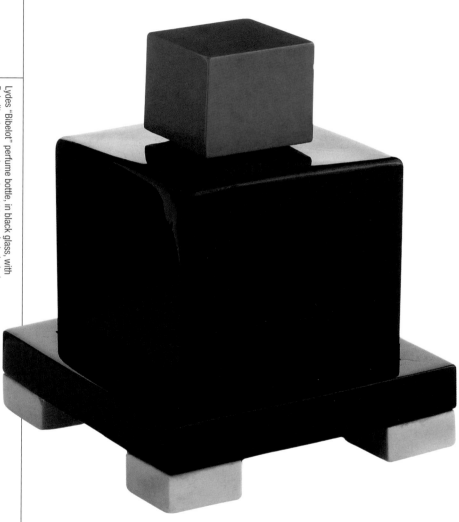

Lydes "Bibelot" perfume bottle, in black glass, with Bakelite stopper and stand. *1920s* ★★★☆☆

F. Millot "Crêpe de Chine" perfume bottle set, comprising eau de cologne and perfume. *1920s* ★ ☆ ☆ ☆

F. Millot "Crêpe de Chine" perfume bottle with box. *1930s* ★ ☆ ☆ ☆

Molinard "Habanita" perfume bottle, with box. *1920s* ★☆☆☆☆

Molinard "Muguet" perfume tester bottle, in clear glass, sealed with a label. *1920s* ★☆☆☆☆

Ota "Bouquet" perfume presentation, of black glass and pearl-finished bottles, in display box with label. *1920s* ★★★★★

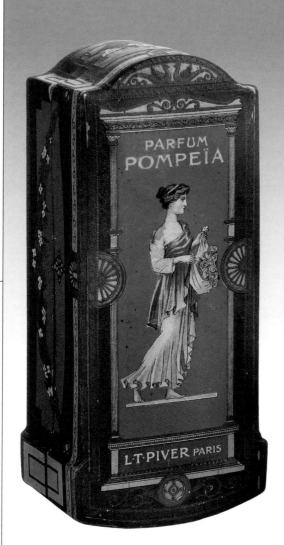

L.T. Piver "Parfum Pompeïa" perfume bottle, with label and shaped box. *1920s* ★★☆☆☆

Potter & Moore "Mitcham Lavender" perfume bottle, in clear glass and plastic. *1920s* ★★ ☆☆☆

Prince Matchabelli "Princess Maria" perfume bottle, in opaque white glass with gold detail and label. *1930s* ★★☆☆☆

Prince Matchabelli "Wing Song" perfume bottle. ★ ☆ ☆ ☆

Small Prince Matchabelli crown-shaped perfume bottle, with gilt decoration. *1920s* ★ ☆ ☆ ☆ ☆

Revillon "Carnel de Bal" perfume bottle, shaped like inverted whiskey glass, with gold label. *1930s* ★☆☆☆☆

Revillon "Amou Daria" perfume bottle; square, masculine,
geometric design is classically 1930s, unlike feminine
1920s styles. *1930s* ★ ☆☆☆☆

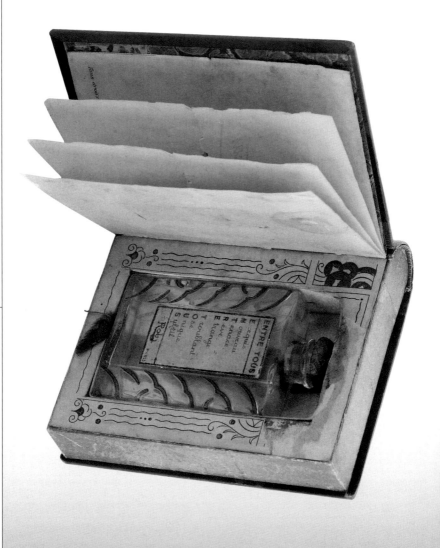

Robj "Entre Tous" perfume bottle with sepia stain and label, in book-shaped box. *1920s* ★★★☆☆

Rosine "Aladin" perfume bottle in cast metal, with chain handle and faux ivory stopper. ★ ★ ☆ ☆ ☆

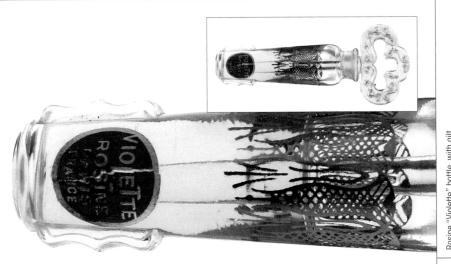

Rosine "Violette" bottle, with gilt decoration and large, key-shaped stopper. *1920s* ★ ☆ ☆ ☆ ☆

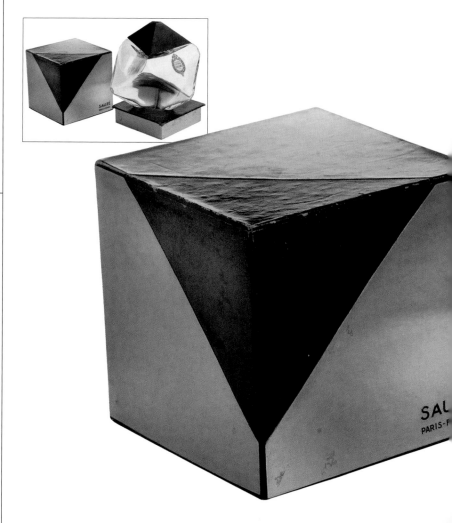

Sauze "Chypre" perfume bottle in clear glass, with Bakelite cover and card display box. ★★★★☆

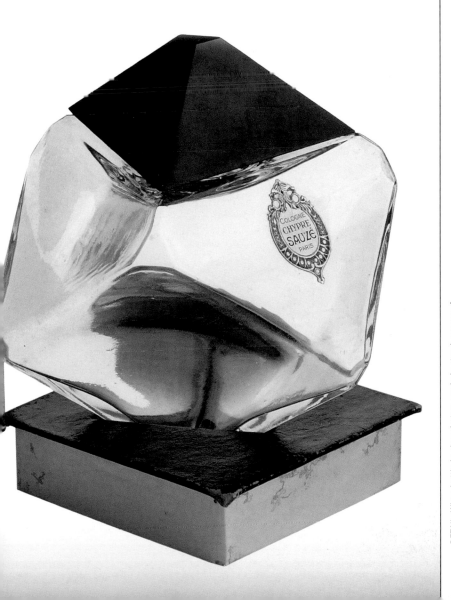

DETAIL: When bottle is placed at an angle in stand, corner of cube becomes the cap.

COLOGNE
CHYPRE
SAUZÉ
PARIS

SCHIAPARELLI

Italian-born fashion designer Elsa Schiaparelli (1890–1973) was known for her radical and witty clothing, inspired by modern and surrealist art. She experimented with new materials such as cellophane and zippers; in addition, she created accessories in the shapes of lamb cutlets, snails, and folded newspapers.

Schiaparelli's unique take on design was evident in her perfume bottles. The 1936 bottle for "Shocking" was shaped like a female torso and inspired by Mae West, for whom Schiaparelli designed clothes. "Zut" was sold in a container shaped like a woman's hips and legs, with a skirt around the ankles. While most Schiaparelli bottles are sought-after today, her "Le Roi Soleil," topped with a gilded stopper shaped as a sun and designed by Salvador Dali, is especially desirable.

Schiaparelli "Shocking" perfume bottle in domed presentation, with box. *1930s* ★ ★ ☆ ☆ ☆

Miniature Schiaparelli sample perfume bottle, in the form of a female torso. ★★☆☆☆

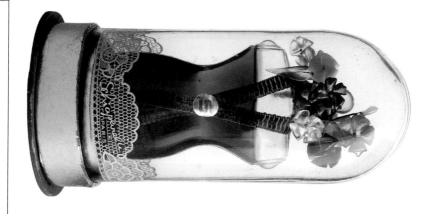

Schiaparelli 'Shocking" perfume in domed presentation, shaped like a dressmaker's dummy with tape measure. *1930s* ★★☆☆☆

Schiaparelli "Shocking" miniature perfume bottle, shaped like a female torso, under plastic dome.   *1930s*   ★ ★ ☆ ☆ ☆

Set of Schiaparelli "Shocking" perfume bottles with screw caps, in animated "Shock-in-the-Box" presentation box. *1930s* ★★☆☆☆

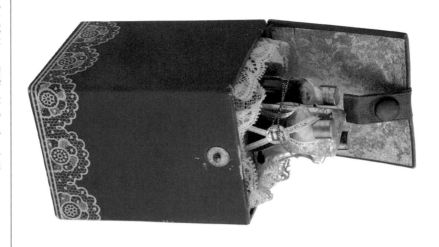

Schiaparelli "Shocking" perfume bottle in special "Spin & Win" presentation: four miniature bottles revolve when box lid pops up. *1930s* ★★★★☆

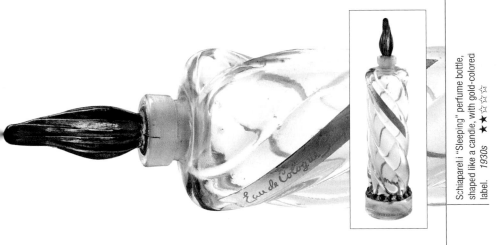

Schiaparelli "Sleeping" perfume bottle, shaped like a candle, with gold-colored label. *1930s* ★ ★ ☆ ☆ ☆

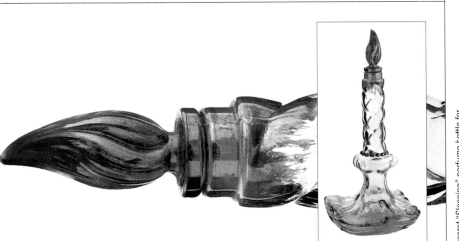

Baccarat "Sleeping" perfume bottle for Schiaparelli, in clear and red crystal with gilded details. *1930s* ★ ★ ☆ ☆ ☆

CREATURE FEATURE

p.302

p.385

p.176

p.283

p.282

p.282

p.157

p.344

p.102

p.265

p.282

p.128

p.145

p.375

p.353

p.383

CREATURE FEATURE

Schuco novelty perfume bottle shaped like a plush fabric bear, with glass tube insert. *1920s* ★☆☆☆☆

Schuco novelty perfume bottle shaped like a plush fabric monkey in a top hat, with glass tube insert. *1920s* ★★☆☆☆

Schuco teddy bear perfume bottle in brown mohair, with orange glass eyes and black plastic nose. ★☆☆☆☆

Schuco novelty perfume bottle with glass tube insert and rare Schuco hang tag. *1920s* ★★☆☆☆

DETAIL: Opened toy, showing bottle.

Schuco novelty perfume bottle shaped like a plush fabric monkey with glass tube insert *1920s* ★★☆☆☆

Steuben perfume bottle in green jade. *1920s* ★★☆☆

Steuben Aurene perfume bottle in iridescent blue, with matching stopper. ★★☆☆

Steuben scent bottle in dark green, in shape "1455." ★★☆☆

Steuben scent bottle in iridescent white, in shape "1455." ★★☆☆

STEUBEN

The Steuben company was founded in 1903 in Corning, Steuben County, New York, by Frederick Carder, an innovative designer and glass technologist. The company became famous for its iridescent art glass during the early 20th century, and by 1920 was producing elegant modern perfume bottles and atomizers.

In 1904, Carder patented his "Gold Aurene" range, which became an instant success, challenging Tiffany's Favrile ware. New finishes, including "Blue Aurene," "Red Aurene," and "Verre de Soie," were soon introduced. Forms were typically conventional, and included footed bowls, squat vases, and twisted candlesticks. Some pieces were enhanced with pulled decoration, although in many cases their beauty lay in the even sheen of the iridescent surface. Following the development of a new lead crystal in 1932, the company made elegant, clear, cut glass. Carder was to design over 6,000 different pieces for Steuben, and continued to experiment with new techniques until he retired at the age of 96.

★ ★ ★ ★ ☆

Steuben green jade perfume bottle with clear crystal twisted stopper. ★ ☆☆☆☆

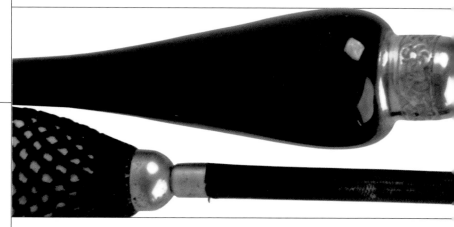

Steuben black amethyst atomizer. ★ ☆☆☆☆

Steuben blue Aurene atomizer in iridescent blue, with intaglio-cut design of flowers and leaves. ★★★☆☆

Steuben blue Aurene perfume bottle. ★★★★☆

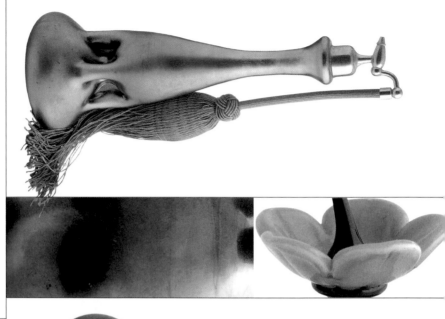

Steuben blue Aurene perfume bottle with unusual black and pink, flower-shaped stopper. ★★★★☆

Rare Suzy "Ecarlette Suzy" miniature perfume bottle, with plastic screw cap shaped as hat. *1930s* ★★☆☆

J. Viard "Magda" perfume bottle for Lubin, in clear and frosted glass with gold details. *1920s* ★★★★☆

J. Viard "Qui m'aime?" perfume bottle for Best & Co., with gold label, glass beads, and box. *1920s* ★★☆☆☆

Depincix perfume bottle, designed by J. Viard for Dubarry, in clear and frosted glass with stained and painted details. ★★★☆ ★★★

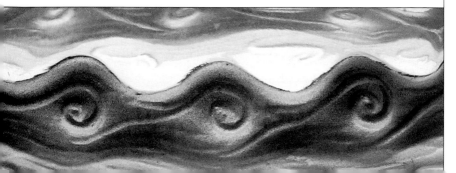

Clear glass perfume bottle, possibly by Viard, with blue glass decoration and atomizer with replaced tassel. *1920s* ★☆☆☆☆

Depinoix "Femme Divine" perfume bottle, by Viard for Loulette, with pink enamel and gray stain. *1920s* ★★☆☆☆

Viard "Ambre de Carthage" perfume bottle for Isabey,
in clear and frosted glass with gray stain and faux
Spanish leather box.   *1920s*   ★★★☆☆

VIARD

Julien Viard's background as a sculptor is evident in the shapely perfume bottles he designed for a wide range of perfumers and glass manufacturers during the early 20th century. Lubin, Dubarry, and D'Orsay, as well as other important companies, commissioned the artist to create glamorous and sophisticated presentations that would enhance the appeal of their fragrances.

The typically graceful shapes were sometimes decorated with frosted glass, picked out with dark shading, and many bottles featured Art Deco designs such as female nudes or exotic Egyptian motifs. Bottles such as "Magda" for Lubin, featuring a woman's head to the stopper and named after the play starring Sarah Bernhardt, are extremely popular with enthusiasts today, and can fetch surprisingly high prices. The card boxes that contained the bottles were often almost as beautiful, and an original box can significantly increase value.

J. Viard "Vers la Joie" perfume bottle for Rigaud, in clear glass with purple stain and gilt details. *1920s* ★★★★☆

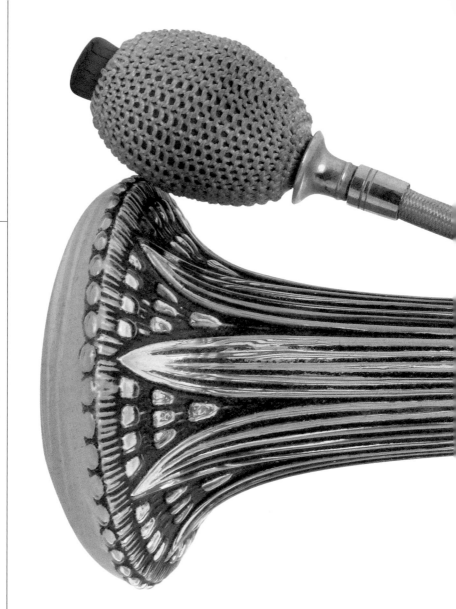

Viard atomizer, with puffer. *1930s* ★ ☆☆☆☆

*"Hast thou not learn'd me how
To make perfumes? distil? preserve? yea, so
That our great king himself doth woo me oft
For my confections?"*

WILLIAM SHAKESPEARE, CYMBELINE

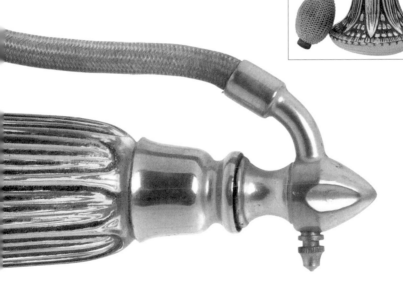

Vigny holiday perfume bottle, shaped as a golly with glass head and plastic screw cap collar, in ornamental box. *1930s* ★★☆☆☆

Two Vigny perfume bottles, shaped as gollies with original hair and labels, based on the character created by Florence K. Upton in 1895. *1930s* ★★★☆☆

Vigny "Good Luck" metal perfume pin, shaped like a golly, with hinged screen on reverse for scented cotton; mounted or card. *1920s* ★★☆☆☆

Vigny "Jack, Jill, and Junior" perfume presentation of clear and black glass bottles with enamel and fur details, in display box. *1920s* ★★★☆

Vigny "Le Chick-Chick" perfume bottle, in clear glass with gold detail. *1920s* ★★☆☆☆

Weil "Antilope" perfume bottle, with engraved "W" on stopper. *1930s* ★ ☆☆☆☆

Worth "Vers Le Jour" perfume bottle, in clear glass, with squared shape. *1920s* ★ ☆☆☆☆

Ybry "**Mon Ame**" perfume bottle, in purple crystal with stopper, metal cover, and tasseled box. *1920s* ★ ★ ☆ ☆ ☆

ART DECO

The Art Deco period lasted from the early 1920s to the beginning of the Second World War, and influenced the design of everything from toasters to buildings to perfume bottles. Shapes were geometric, bold, and angular. Inspiration came from Far Eastern and African design, and exotic motifs, such as stylized flowers, sunbursts, blocky borders, and angular swatches adorned the surfaces of perfume bottles. Following the discovery of Tutankhamen's tomb in 1922, sphinx heads or Egyptian-inspired decoration was quite popular. At the same time, new materials, innovative designs, and a need for economy during the Great Depression lead to streamlined, simple forms. The influence of modern architecture, such as the Rockefeller Center in New York, can be seen in the blocky forms and tiered outlines of some bottles.

Art Deco Lucite perfume bottle with skyscraper tiers. ★★☆☆☆

Clear glass perfume bottle with black geometric decoration. *1920s* ★☆☆☆☆

French perfume atomizer purse set with compact ard pill box, in brass with celluloid decoration. *1920s* ★★☆☆

Perfume bottle with "Oeillet" label. 1930s ★☆☆☆

Glass perfume bottle with silver-mounted cover and Royal Worcester plaque, painted by James Stinton. *1920s* ★★☆☆☆

Silver perfume bottle with ridged sides and serpent and spider on cap. *1920s* ★☆☆☆☆

Cut-glass atomizer with stepped sides and painted decoration. *1930s* ★☆☆☆☆

Art Deco green glass perfume bottle with silver stopper and classically chic, streamlined shape. *1920s* ★★☆☆☆

ATOMIZERS

p.112

p.236

p.246

p.251

p.236

p.289

p.288

p.290

p.299

p.294

p.199

p.314

p.316

p.311

p.198

p.317

ATOMIZERS

"Saturday Night" lotion bottle with gold label embossed "ASJ," probably English.
1930s ★ ☆☆☆☆

Clear glass perfume bottle with angular body and black puffer. *1920s* ★ ☆☆☆☆

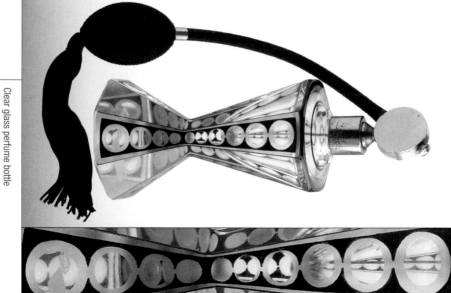

Clear glass perfume bottle and stopper with black geometric design. *1920s* ★☆☆☆☆

French glass perfume bottle with stopper and metallic gold case. *1930s* ★☆☆☆

Clear glass atomizer with overlaid flower decoration. *1930s* ★★☆☆☆

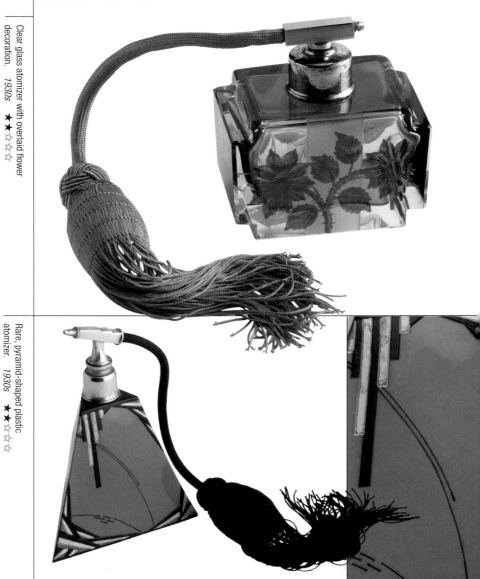

Rare, pyramid-shaped plastic atomizer. *1930s* ★★☆☆☆

Atomizer in cut crystal, with acid-etched enamel in red and yellow geometric design. *1930s* ★★☆☆

Green cut-glass atomizer, suspended from a silver-gilt frame. *1920s* ★☆☆☆

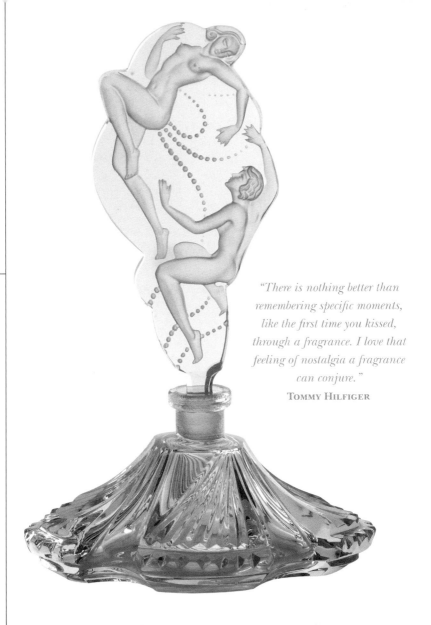

Clear glass perfume bottle, with design of dancing female figures on stopper. *1920s* ★★☆☆☆

"There is nothing better than remembering specific moments, like the first time you kissed, through a fragrance. I love that feeling of nostalgia a fragrance can conjure."

TOMMY HILFIGER

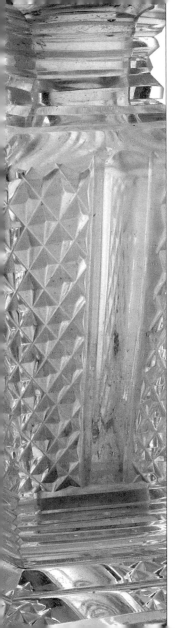

ART DECO STYLE

English glass perfume bottle with silver
Egyptian sarcophagus head; marked
"Senco." *1920s* ★ ☆☆☆☆

Pair of amethyst cut-glass perfume bottles, with matching powder jar. *1930s* ★ ☆☆☆☆

1940s–1950s

Following the restrictions and austerity of WWII, the late 1940s and 1950s saw a surge in demand for bright, feminine fragrances in frivolous and glamorous packaging. Christian Dior's New Look ushered in a return to femininity, while Chanel's chic suits continued to influence styles. Lancôme, Balenciaga, and Nina Ricci launched sophisticated new perfumes, and Guerlain and Schiaparelli remained popular.

The post-war years saw a general decline in the quality of many bottles, and machine-ground glass and plastic screw caps became common. Manufacturers compensated for cheap materials by marketing eye-catching bottles in novelty shapes. Max Factor released a range of scents in velour cat-shaped bottles with diamanté eyes, and Elizabeth Arden produced seasonal gift presentation sets. Lilly Daché enjoyed success with her fragrances in bottles shaped as poodles, a fashionable design motif of the period.

Balenciaga "Quadrille" perfume bottle, with plastic lid and embossed leather slip case. *1950s* ★☆☆☆☆

Caron "Les Pois de Senteur de Chez Moi" perfume bottle, with fitted box. *1940s* ★ ★ ☆ ☆ ☆

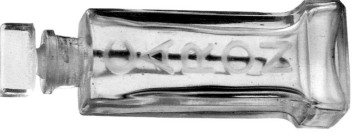

Two Caron "Voeu de Noel" perfume tester bottles: one with label, one etched "Caron." *1940s* ★ ☆ ☆ ☆ ☆

POST-WAR ELEGANCE

During the Second World War, rationing and government legislation meant that the variety of clothing and accessories on sale was severely limited. After the exuberance of the 1930s, fashionable women had to "make do and mend" by sewing their own outfits out of discarded fabric, or buying dresses in drab tones and simple cuts off the peg. Perfume bottles too were plain, a huge contrast to the lavish packaging with which customers had become familiar.

In 1947, Christian Dior (1905–57) launched the "New Look," a style that was to remain influential for a decade. Practical wartime clothing made from economical fabrics was replaced with indulgent, generously cut outfits that were feminine and sophisticated. Net petticoats and rigid undergarments helped create the distinctive silhouette. At the same time, his new fragrance "Miss Dior" was sold in an elegant bottle that complemented the style.

Christian Dior "Miss Dior" perfume bottle. This classic 1940s design was inspired by a Grecian urn. *1940s* ★ ☆ ☆ ☆ ☆

De Raymond "Pinx" perfume bottle in "Christmas Tree" holiday presentation, with plastic display box.   *1940s*   ★★☆☆☆

Elizabeth Arden "Blue Grass" bottle in "Merry Christmas Stocking" presentation. *1950s* ★ ★ ☆ ☆ ☆

Elizabeth Arden "Parfums par Noël" presentation, containing blown glass bottles of "Cyclamen," "Night & Day," and "Blue Grass" hung in net stockings. *1940s* ★★★★☆

1940s–1950s

Two Goya "Gardenia" perfume bottle, one containing some original perfume, with box. *1950s* ★☆☆☆☆

Goya "21" perfume bottle. An original box,
especially one with stylish period graphics, makes
bottles more valuable.   *1950s*   ★ ☆ ☆ ☆

GORGEOUS GIFTS

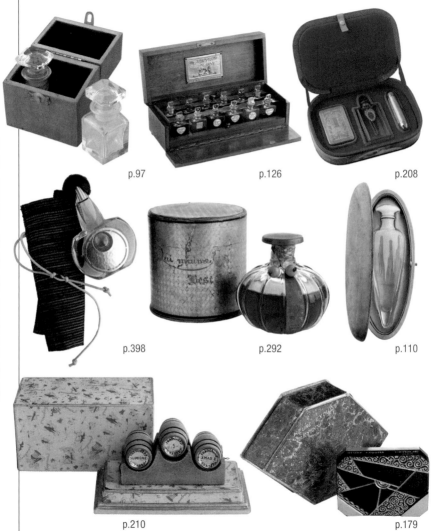

p.97

p.126

p.208

p.398

p.292

p.110

p.210

p.179

p.297

p.352

p.328

p.104

p.329

p.250

p.180

"I felt something so intense, I could only express it in a perfume."

JACQUES GUERLAIN

Guerlain "Jicky" perfume bottle in French opaline crystal with bronze neck and gilt stopper, signed by R. Noirot. *1950s* ★★★★★☆

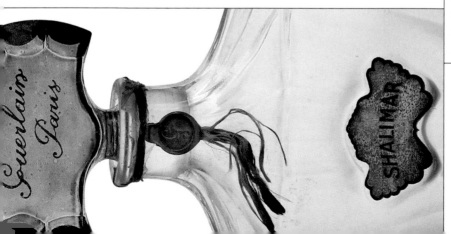

Guerlain "Shalimar" perfume bottle, named after the gardens that the Mughal emperor Shah Jahan created in 1641 for his wife. *1950s* ★ ☆ ☆ ☆

Hattie Carnegie "Perfume Hypnotic" miniature perfume bottle, in clear glass with gold detail. *1940s* ★☆☆☆☆

The engraved stopper has a ring so that the bottle can be hung on a chain around the wearer's neck.

☆☆☆☆☆
★

Lancôme "Magie de Lancôme" perfume bottle, in the form of a pendant. *1950s*

1940s–1950s

Lancôme "Tropiques" limited-edition perfume bottle designed by Jean Sala, in clear and frosted glass, with display box. *1940s* ★★★☆☆

"Happiness is like perfume;
you can't give it away without
getting a little on yourself."
ANON

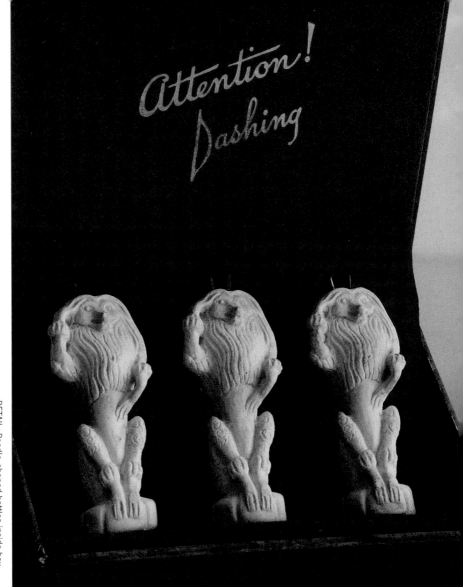

DETAIL: Poodle-shaped bottles inside box.

LILLY DACHÉ

Born on a rural French farm, Lilly Daché (1898–1989) went on to set the New York fashion world alight. As a rebellious youngster, she left the farm to train as a milliner, under the guidance of her aunt, before emigrating to the US at the age of 25. After briefly working as a shop assistant, she purchased a small New York hat store. It was not long before her innovative designs attracted the attention of fashionable socialites. In 1929, she married the Frenchman and Coty employee Jean Després, and the couple worked to expand the thriving company.

In 1941, Daché added perfumes to the rapidly expanding product line. Like her hats and other accessories, her bottles were glamorous and exuberant. Her "Dashing" perfume was packaged in a poodle-shaped container, while "Drifting" was daringly sold in a bottle modeled as a woman's breast.

Set of Lilly Daché "Dashing" miniature perfume bottles, in "Attention!" presentation box.   *1940s*   ★★★★★

Lilly Daché "Dashing" perfume bottle on a silk base with cover; missing stopper. *1940s* ★★★☆☆

*"Fragrance is the invisible cosmetic,
and one of the most personal
and subtle of all."*

LILLY DACHÉ

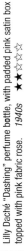

Lilly Daché "Dashing" perfume bottle, with padded pink satin box topped with pink fabric rose. *1940s* ★★☆☆☆

"Childhood smells of perfume and brownies."

DAVID LEAVITT

Lucien Lelong "Castle" presentation of perfumes comprising "Mon Image," "Tailspin," "Lilac," and "Honeysuckle," with plastic castle in display box. *1940s* ★☆☆☆☆

POTS OF FUN

p.352

p.108

p.66

p.358

p.267

p.266

p.201

p.270

p.277

p.372

POTS OF FUN

p.173

p.350

p.434

p.61

p.229

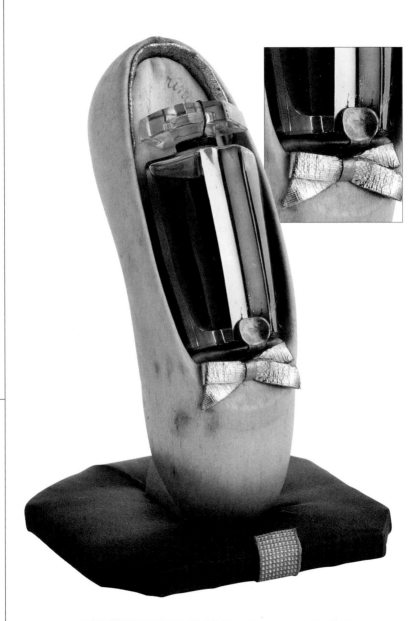

Marie Earl "Ballerina" perfume bottle in clear glass with gilded detail, in ballet shoe presentation. *1940s* ★★★★☆

Marquay "Prince Douka" perfume bottle in clear and frosted glass, with jeweled fabric cape and label. *1950s* ★ ★ ☆ ☆ ☆

Set of Marquay "Prince Douka" perfume bottles in clear and frosted glass, with fabric capes and labels, in plastic display box. *1950s* ★ ★ ☆ ☆ ☆

Mary Chess set of three perfume bottles, designed by Grace Robinson, and manufactured by the Wheaton Glass Company. ★☆☆☆☆

Mary Chess "Perfume Gallery" presentation of six perfumes in glass bottles shaped as chess pieces, with chessboard box. *1950s* ★★☆☆☆

Max Factor "Chantrelle" perfume, in clear, domed box with cat wearing flower collar. *1950s* ★ ☆☆☆☆

Max Factor "Chantrelle" perfume bottle with cat in yellow bow tie. Many variations of the cat presentation were produced. *1950s* ★ ☆☆☆☆

NINA RICCI

Although Nina Ricci (1883–1970) was in her 50s when she opened her own couture house, she rapidly built up a worldwide fashion empire. Born in Turin, Italy, Ricci was apprenticed to a dressmaker at the age of 13. After working as a designer for Raffin from 1908, she finally set up on her own in 1932. Her outfits, aimed at sophisticated, more mature ladies, were glamorous and flattering, although fairly traditional.

In 1946, Ricci's son Robert Ricci established "Parfums Nina Ricci," the fragrance arm of the company. Nina Ricci's first perfume was "Coeur Joie," and Robert Ricci turned to Lalique to design the heart-shaped bottle. The classic "L'Air du Temps," meaning "mood of the times," also designed by Lalique, was released in 1949 and the famous bottle with its dove stopper was introduced in 1951. The scent remains an international bestseller, and the company continues to thrive today.

Nina Ricci "Coeur Joie" perfume bottle, with box. *1940s* ★ ☆☆☆☆☆

Nina Ricci "Coeur Joie" perfume bottle, designed by Lalique. This bottle would be more valuable with a label. ★☆☆☆☆

Nina Ricci "Coeur Joie" perfume bottle with three heart-shaped motifs and gold-plated stopper. *1940s* ★☆☆☆☆

Nina Ricci "Coeur Joie"
perfume bottle, designed by
Lalicue. *1940s* ★ ☆ ☆ ☆

Raphael "Republique" perfume bottle, designed by Lalique, shaped like a pinecone. *1940s* ★☆☆☆☆

Renoir "Chichi" heart-shaped perfume bottle, made in France for US market. *1940s* ★☆☆☆☆

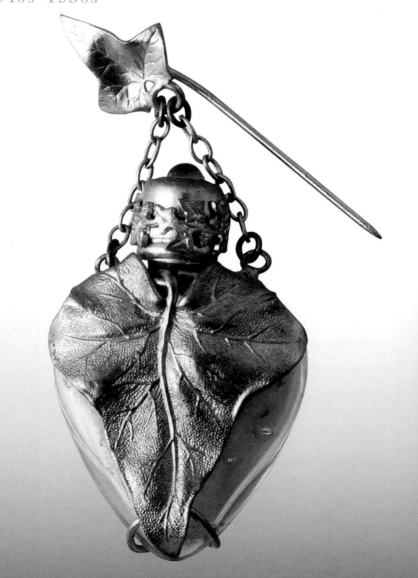

Rare Schiaparelli "Succès Fou" perfume bottle pin, in gilded metal set with glass cabochons. *1940s* ★★★★☆

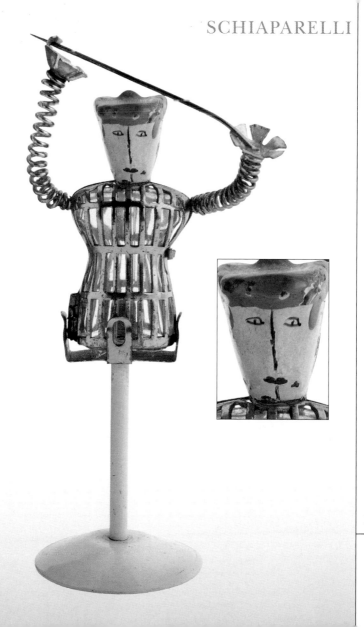

Schiaparelli "Shocking Scamp" presentation of "Shocking" perfume: miniature bottle held in metal brooch, on metal stand. *1940* ★★★☆

NOVELTY BOTTLES

The novelty perfume bottle has a long history. Nobles of the 16th century carried pomanders shaped as nuts or skulls, while 200 years later, wealthy individuals owned mandolin- or boot-shaped bottles. The market for unusual bottles remained strong throughout the Victorian period and into the 20th century, as exciting glass crowns by Prince Matchabelli competed with the hour-glass figure designs of Schiaparelli.

The development of Bakelite in the 1930s gave manufacturers a new material to play with and meant that experimental packaging could be produced at a lower price. The best-selling "Evening in Paris" by Bourjois was brought out in Bakelite containers shaped as on owl, a clock, and a hotel door, and Lionceau released "La Saison des Fleurs" perfume solids in novelty dice containers. Other popular novelty bottles included Lilly Daché's dog-shaped bottles and toymaker Schuco's cuddly teddy bear containers with plush fur.

Schiaparelli "Zut" perfume bottle in clear and frosted glass with gold details, and with silk-lined box. *1940s* ★ ★ ☆ ☆ ☆

Pair of Schiaparelli display lamps for Place Vendôme salon, with painted vellum shades; bases are glass "Sleeping" perfume bottles. ★★★☆☆

This risqué bottle is shaped like a woman's hips and legs, with a skirt around her ankles.

Schiaparelli "Zut" perfume bottle, with gilt decoration and ribbon sash. ★★ ☆☆☆

Schiaparelli "Zut" perfume bottle, in clear and frosted glass with gold details and suede pouch. Bottle is shaped as a woman's legs, with skirt around ankles. *1940s* ★★☆☆☆

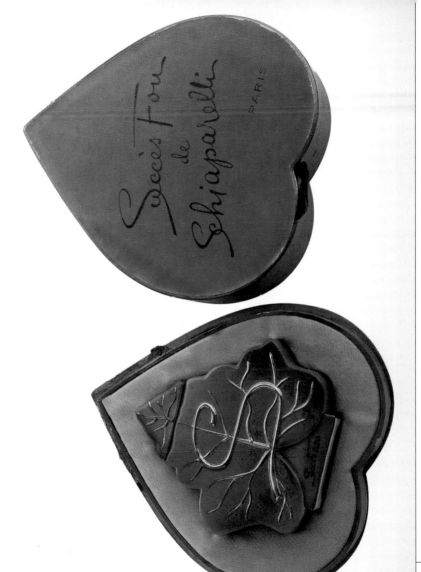

Schiaparelli "Success Fou" perfume bottle, in white glass with foil label and gilt detail. *1950s* ★ ★ ☆ ☆ ☆

SCHIAPARELLI

p.277

p.275

p.276

p.276

p.366

p.364

p.279

p.367

p.278

p.278

p.279

p.363

p.370

Schiaparelli "Shocking You" Perfume bottle, with novelty cigarette carton box. *1940s* ★☆☆☆☆

*"In difficult times, fashion
is always outrageous."*
ELSA SCHIAPARELLI

Tuvache "Ze Zan" perfume bottle in gilt glass, with striking, gold-glazed ceramic display cover. *1940s* ★★★★★☆

DETAIL: Gilt glass bottle with wooden screw cap and stand.

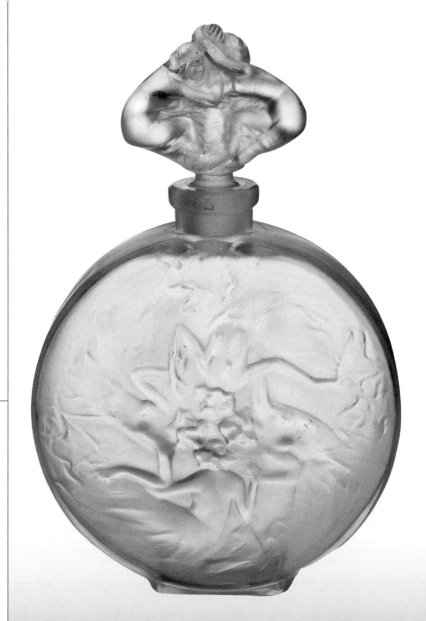

Lalique "Rosace Figurines" perfume bottle, originally designed in 1912, in clear and frosted glass. *1940s*
★★★★☆

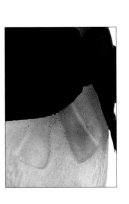

Very rare French glass cat perfume bottle, by
unknown maker; probably 1950s. ★

☆☆☆☆

*"I'm inspired by gardens, nature, travel,
and women. I created all my perfumes for
women I admire or have loved."*

JEAN-PAUL GUERLAIN

FIGURES & FLOWERS

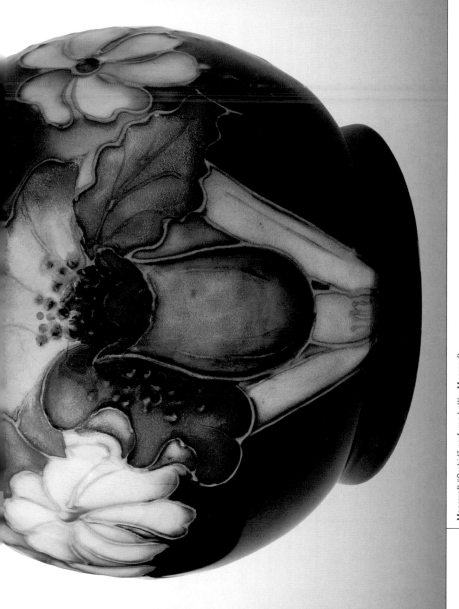

Moorcroft "Orchid" perfume bottle. Moorcroft pottery, typically decorated with floral designs, is widely collected today. *1950s* ★★☆☆☆

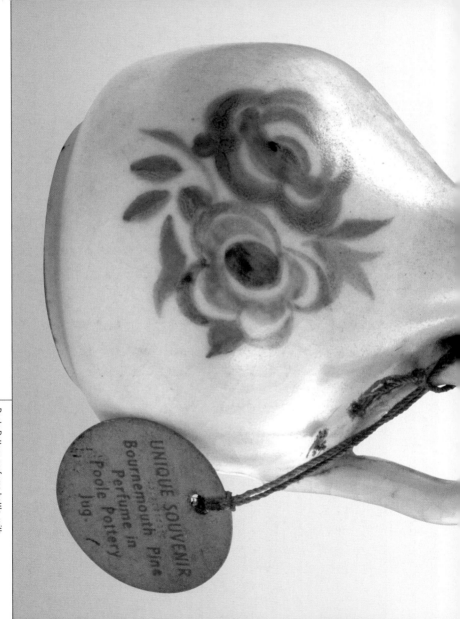

Poole Pottery perfume bottle, with label for "W.H. Smiths, The Square, Bournemouth." ★ ☆ ☆ ☆ ☆

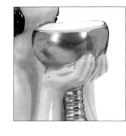

Porcelain electric perfume burner shaped as kneeling woman. 1950s ☆☆☆☆ ★

1960s– PRESENT

During the 1960s and 1970s, luxury perfume presentations were increasingly replaced by inexpensive bottles of little design merit. The expansion of the youth market meant manufacturers were forced to keep costs down and designs up to date. Avon dominated the lower end of the market, while established perfumers such as Guerlain, and fashion houses such as Hermès, remained popular with wealthier customers. Solid perfume in decorative cases also enjoyed a brief period of popularity.

During the 1980s, big name brands, such as Dior and Yves St Laurent, dominated the perfume market and released heavy perfumes in striking packaging that suited the tastes of the time. Lighter, fresher scents, including "Eternity" by Calvin Klein, complemented the casual look and laid-back attitude of the 1990s, as did unisex perfumes such as "CK One."

AVON

When door-to-door Bible salesman David H. McConnell found that a free perfume sample offered with each purchase was more popular with American housewives than his books, he knew he had a great business idea. Avon, famous for its strategy of selling cosmetics on the doorstep, was established in 1886 as the Californian Perfume Company. A visit to the picturesque English town of Stratford-upon-Avon during the 1930s prompted McConnell to change the name to something he felt was less regional. By this time, over 25,000 sales representatives were selling the company's perfumes and other beauty products all over the world.

Avon perfume bottles, particularly mass-produced examples dating from the 1960s and later, remain affordable. Some bottles can be picked up for next to nothing, but interest in the area is growing rapidly and rare items are starting to fetch higher prices.

Basket-shaped Avon pin containing perfume wax, in gold-washed metal with hinged lid and clear rhinestone highlights. *1970s* ★☆☆☆☆

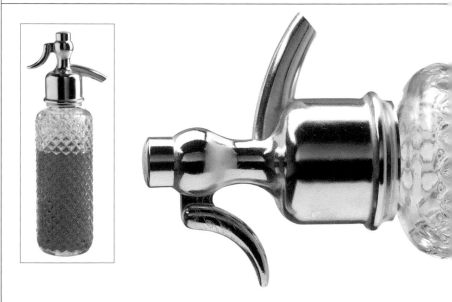

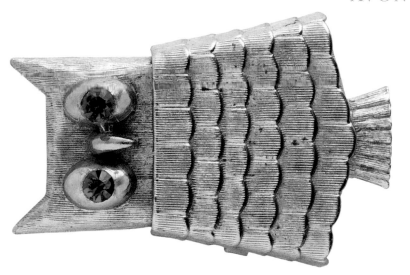

Owl-shaped Avon pin holding perfume wax, in gold-washed metal with hinged lid and emerald-green rhinestone eyes. *1970s* ★ ☆☆☆☆

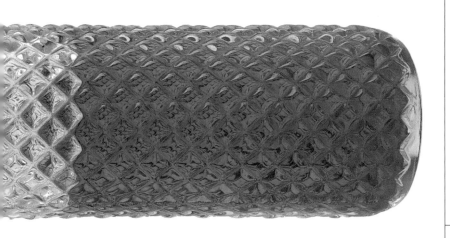

Large Avon perfume bottle shaped like a soda siphon. *1960s* ★ ☆☆☆☆

Balmain "Jolie Madame" perfume bottle, introduced in 1957. ★☆☆☆☆

"A perfume is more than an extract, it is a presence in abstraction. A perfume, for me, is a mystique."

GIORGIO ARMANI

SO
PRETTY
DE
Cartier
PARFUM
CRISTAL PERLES 3 ORS
50 ml   1.6 fl.oz.

Harrods
KNIGHTSBRIDGE

N° 053 /820

DETAIL: Cartier and Harrods marks on base.

EIGHTIES STYLE

Versace, Dior, Gucci: style in the 1980s meant brand names and designer labels. Great fashion houses and high-profile designers advertised exciting new perfumes with big-budget poster campaigns, and were rewarded with healthy profits that helped bolster the income from their clothing lines. Looking for new ways to increase sales, Giorgio Beverly Hills pioneered the use of scented strips in magazines. Power-dressed executives snapped up bottles of Yves St. Laurent's "Opium," Dior's "Poison," and Calvin Klein's "Obsession," many of which were bought in duty-free shops after a trip abroad.

The 1990s saw a move away from the power and money-focused 1980s with the release of lighter scents, such as "L'Eau d'Issey" by Issey Miyake and "CK One" by Calvin Klein.

Limited-edition Cartier "So Pretty" perfume in "Three Gold Pearls" bottle, with Harrods box. *1990s* ★ ★ ☆ ☆ ☆

David Salazar "Angelfish" perfume bottle. Salazar invented "painting with glass": "drawing" on a hot glass surface with a heated glass rod. ★☆☆☆☆

☆☆★
★★★

Fabergé crystal perfume bottle, made exclusively by
Cristallerie St. Louis of France.

Guerlain "Chant d'Arômes" perfume bottle in frosted and clear glass, with rosebud-shaped stopper. *1960s* ★☆☆☆☆

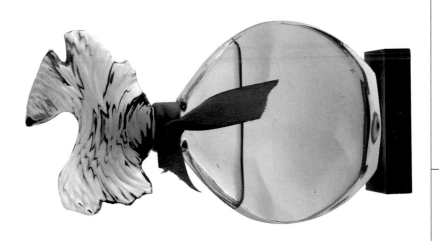

GUERLAIN

From "Mitsouko" to "Samsara," Guerlain has been responsible for some of the most memorable perfumes of the last 150 years. Chemist and doctor Pierre-François Guerlain founded the company in 1828, and established himself as a leading perfumer by selling customized fragrances to wealthy Parisians. In 1853, he was appointed perfumer to the Court of Napoleon III and created "Eau Imperiale" for the Empress.

Pierre Guerlain's sons Aimé and Gabriel took over the company in 1890 and introduced the popular "Jicky," one of the first perfumes to contain synthetic oils, later that decade. Jacques Guerlain, Gabriel's son, was appointed in the early 20th century and took the company to new heights. Known as one of the greatest perfumers of the century, he was responsible for "Mitsouko," "L'Heure Bleue," and "Shalimar." Over the years, more than 200 different perfumes have been introduced, in a large variety of attractive bottles. The company continues to thrive today.

Guerlain "Vol de Nuit" perfume bottle with plastic stopper, in zebra-pattern printed box. *1960s* ★ ☆☆☆☆

Guerlain "Jardins de Bagatelle" perfume bottle. This perfume was introduced in 1983. *1980s* ★★★☆☆

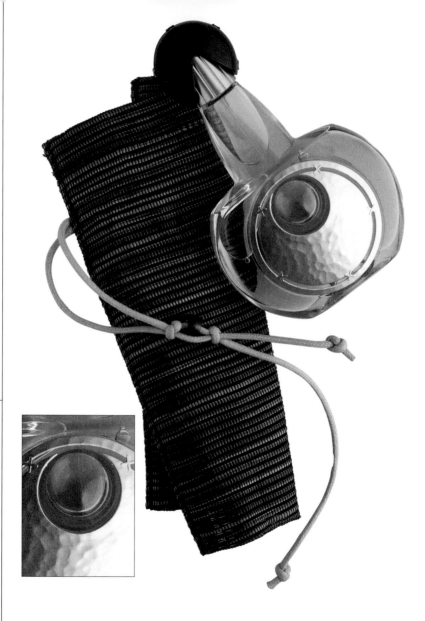

Guerlain "Mahora" perfume bottle, with applied disk in hammered gold, and original bag. *1980s* ★☆☆☆☆

Guerlain "Guerlinade" perfume bottle, signed by Jean-Paul Guerlain. This 1922 perfume was re-released in 1989 to mark the company's bicentenary. ★ ☆☆☆☆

GLORIOUSLY GIRLY

p.64

p.417

p.192

p.393

p.333

p.392

p.345

p.389

p.59

p.395

p.30

p.28

p.16

p.367

p.95

p.153

Hermès "Calèche" perfume bottle, with box containing silk Hermès cushion; introduced in 1961. ★☆☆☆☆

"The barge she sat in, like a burnished throne,
Burned on the water: the poop was beaten gold;
Purple the sails, and so perfumed that
The winds were lovesick with them"

WILLIAM SHAKESPEARE
(ANTONY AND CLEOPATRA)

DETAIL: Polished base with square black label.

MODERN GLASS

From the 1950s onward, the world of art glass was reinvigorated as makers began experimenting with radical new forms and techniques. The growth in interest in studio glass allowed a huge array of designers to create exciting new designs for perfume bottles. US glassmakers such as Michael Nourot and David Salaza, as well as many others, produced handcrafted bottles alongside other ranges of decorative and functional glass. The traditional technique of glassblowing was used in original ways to make striking modern forms.

Michael Harris was the force behind the popular British glass company Isle of Wight Glass. Having extended his skills at Mdina glassworks in Malta, Harris produced a wide range of colorful glass on the small island off the south coast of England. Gold and silver foil decoration is typical of his thin and finely blown work.

Isle of Wight studio glass "Victorian" perfume bottle. *1990s* ★ ☆☆☆☆☆

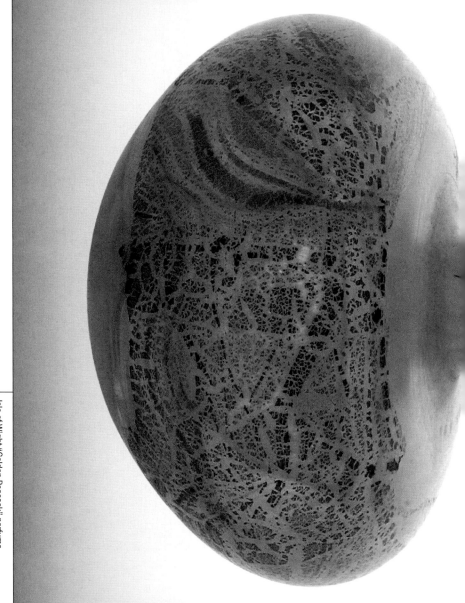

Isle of Wight "Golden Peacock" perfume bottle, with white ground and gold foil decoration. *1980s* ★☆☆☆☆

DETAIL: "Isle of Wight Glass" sticker on base.

DETAIL: Risqué poster for Jean-Paul Gaultier's fragrance "Classique."

JEAN-PAUL GAULTIER

The couturier Jean-Paul Gaultier (born 1952) has become one of the most important designers of recent years. After working for Pierre Cardin and Jean Patou, Gaultier set up his own label in 1972, and produced playful designs influenced by street fashion, surrealism, fetishism, and historical styles. The conical bustier famously worn by Madonna during her 1990 Blonde Ambition tour was one of the most iconic images of the decade. The designer was also responsible for the corset dress, skirts for men, and the costumes in Luc Besson's film *The Fifth Element.*

Gaultier supported his haute couture lines by introducing a range of successful perfumes in striking packaging. His "Le Male" and "Classique" fragrances were launched in torso-shaped bottles, which took inspiration from Schiaparelli's "Shocking," while "Fragile" was sold in a snowdome container. He continues to release limited-edition variations today.

★☆☆☆☆

Jean-Paul Gaultier "Le Male" atomizer bottle.

"Fragrance is the first layer of dressing, a woman's invisible body suit."

DONNA KARAN

Jear.-Paul Gaultier "Fragile" perfume bottle, shaped like a snowdome with tiny female figure.   2001   ★☆☆☆☆

Lalique perfume bottle in original box.   *1980s*   ★☆☆☆☆

Worth "Dans la Nuit" perfume bottle. Originally designed by Lalique in the 1920s, this bottle was reissued in 1985. *1980s* ★ ☆☆☆☆

p.305

p.119

p.285

p.167

p.169

p.436

p.164

p.201

p.260

JOY

DE

JEAN PATOU
Paris

p.232

p.202

p.220

p.202

p.221

p.220

COOL SOPHISTICATION

Lancôme "Magie Noire" perfume bottle, first introduced in 1978. *1980s* ★☆☆☆☆

FLACON CRISTAL TAILLÉ
PYRAMIDE & CRISTAL
ÉDITION NUMÉROTÉE
CRYSTAL CUT NUMBERED EDITION
P A R F U M

Lancôme "Trésor" perfume in "Pyramid & Crystal" perfume bottle, from limited edition of 10,000.   *1980s*   ★ ☆☆☆☆

Small, spherical Mdina glass perfume bottle, with clear stopper; signed on base. *1980s* ★☆☆☆☆

American Michael Nourot glass perfume bottle. *21st century* ★☆☆☆☆

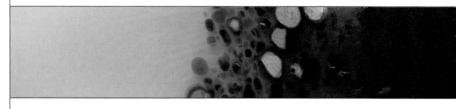

American Michael Nourot glass perfume bottle. *21st century* ★☆☆☆☆

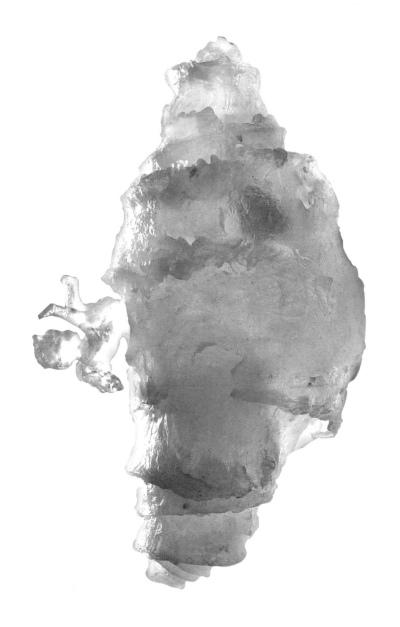

French Michele Pérozeni "Flacon II"
perfume bottle, shaped as cloud with
cherub stopper. ★ ★ ★ ★ ★

Nina Ricci "L'Air du Temps" sample perfume bottle, first introduced in the 1940s, with plastic dove stopper based on an original design by Lalique. ★☆☆☆☆

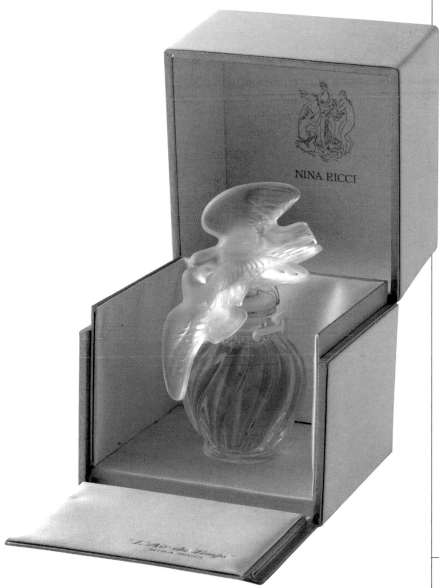

Nina Ricci "L'Air Du Temps" perfume bottle, designed by Lalique. *1970s* ★ ☆☆☆☆

FUTURE CLASSICS

Despite mass-production, the late 20th century was an exciting time for perfume bottles. The star-shaped bottle for Thierry Mugler's "Angel" was one of the most original flasks of the 1990s, and was marketed as being ecologically sound. At the same time, designers were incorporating motifs from their clothing ranges into their perfume packaging. Vivien Westwood's "Boudoir" was released in a bottle topped with her distinctive royal orb emblem, while Jean-Paul Gaultier's male torso bottles wore striped sailor shirts.

As the perfume market became crowded, fashion houses started to release limited-edition fragrances, such as Dior's 2000 "Remember Me," while retailers promoted their scents with special packaging or seasonal gift sets. Oversized dummy "factice" bottles, used for display at perfume counters or in shop windows, are also highly collectable.

Set of three Nina Ricci "Deci Delà" perfume bottles. *1980s* ★☆☆☆☆

"The creation of a perfume is an act of love, whether real or imaginary. I am romantic. I couldn't imagine living without dreams."

NINA RICCI

L'Air du Temps

NINA RICCI

Nina Ricci limited-edition "L'Air du Temps";
"The Winged Bottle" shape was designed
by Lalique. ★ ★ ☆ ☆ ☆

p.295

p.205

p.433

p.233

p.185

p.265

p.232

p.325

p.171

p.90

p.292

p.213

p.105

p.185

p.102

PERFECT PACKAGES

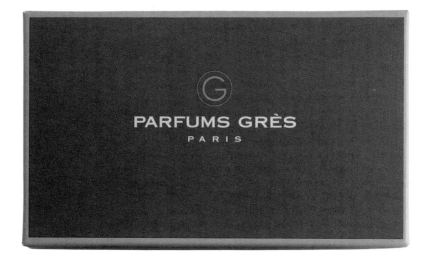

Set of two Parfums Grés perfume bottles: "Cabochard," launched in 1959 when the company started; and "Cabotine," launched in 1990. *1990s* ★ ☆ ☆ ☆

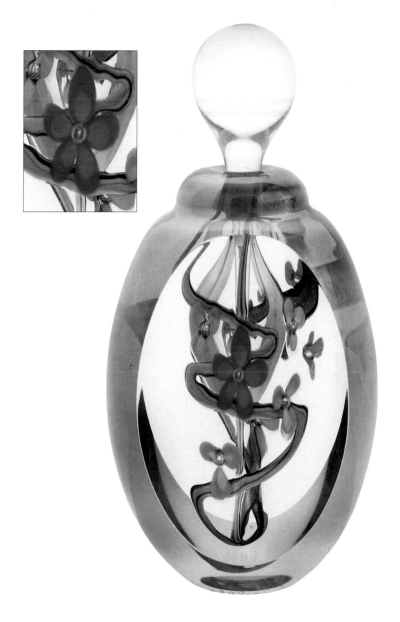

PARFUMS GRÈS / RICHARD GILLIAN

Richard Gillian "Floral with Vines" bottle, with flamework design; dated "2002." ★ ☆☆☆☆

Rochas "Moustache" aftershave bottle. *1970s* ★☆☆☆☆

Rochas "Femme" perfume bottle. *1990s* ★☆☆☆☆

Ultima II "Head Over Heels" perfume bottle, with stopper shaped as a woman's legs; boxed. *1980s* ★ ☆☆☆☆

Van Cleef & Arpels "First" limited-edition perfume bottle. *1990s* ☆☆☆☆ ★

Zellique Studio "Hanging Wisteria" perfume bottle, with "painted flamework" freeform patterns and shapes, signed "J.M. 2001." *2001* ★ ☆ ☆ ☆ ☆

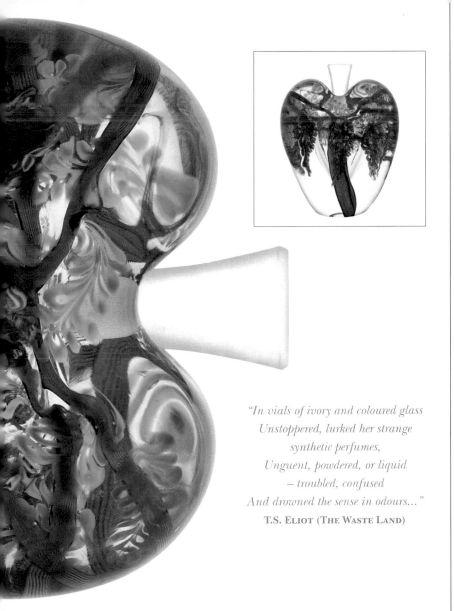

"*In vials of ivory and coloured glass*
Unstoppered, lurked her strange
synthetic perfumes,
Unguent, powdered, or liquid
– troubled, confused
And drowned the sense in odours…"
T.S. ELIOT (THE WASTE LAND)

FLORAL MOTIFS

p.53

p.47

p.378

p.55

p.33

p.336

p.115

p.44

p.377

p.431

p.437

p.227

p.44

p.211

p.161

p.117

p.138

FLORAL MOTIFS

USING THE INTERNET

★ The internet has revolutionized the trading of collectibles as it provides a cost-effective way of buying and selling, away from the overheads of shops and auction rooms. Many millions of collectibles are offered for sale and traded daily, with sites varying from global online marketplaces, such as eBay, to specialist dealers' websites.

★ When searching online, remember that some people may not know how to accurately describe their item. General category searches, even though more time consuming, and even purposefully misspelling a name, can yield results. Also, if something looks too good to be true, it probably is. Using this book to get to know your market visually, so that you can tell the difference between a real bargain and something that sounds like one, is a good start.

★ As you will understand from buying this book, color photography is vital – look for online listings that include as many images as possible and check them carefully. Beware that colors can appear differently, even between computer screens.

★ Always ask the vendor questions about the object, particularly regarding condition. If there is no image, or you want to see another aspect of the object – ask. Most sellers (private or trade) will want to realize the best price for their items so will be more than happy to help – if approached politely and sensibly.

★ As well as the "e-hammer" price, you will probably have to pay additional transactional fees such as packing, shipping, and possibly regional or national taxes. It is always best to ask for an estimate of these additional costs before leaving a bid. This will also help you tailor your bid as you will have an idea of the maximum price the item will cost if you are successful.

★ As well as the well-known online auction sites, such as eBay, there is a host of other online resources for buying and selling, for example fair and auction date listings.

MUSEUMS

FRANCE

**La Magie du Parfum Musée
et Boutique**
18 Avenue de la Libération
04200 Sisteron
Tel: +33 492 34 28 12
www.magieduparfum.fr.fm

International Perfume Museum
8 place du Cours
06130 Grasse
Tel: +33 497 05 58 00
www.museesdegrasse.com

HOLLAND

Nederlands Parfumflessen Museum
Bosstraat 2
1731 SE Winkel
The Netherlands
Tel +31 224 54l 578
www.parfummuseum.nl

JAPAN

Lalique Museum
Hakone
186-1 Sengokuhara, Hakone-machi,
Ashigarashimo-gun, Kanagawa
prefecture, Zip code 250-0631
Tel: +81 460 4 2255
www.lalique-museum.com

SPAIN

Museu del Perfum
Passeig de Gràcia, 39
Barcelona
Tel. +34 93 216 01 21
www.museudelperfum.com

UK

Victoria and Albert Museum
South Kensington
London SW7 2RL
Tel: +44 20 7938 8500
www.vam.ac.uk

Harris Museum
The Market Square, Preston
Lancashire PR1 2PP, UK
Tel: +44 1772 258 248
www.harrismuseum.org.uk

Broadfield House Glass Museum
Compton Drive, Kingswinford
West Midlands DY6 9NS
Tel: +44 1384 812745
www.glassmuseum.org.uk

USA

**The Annette Green Museum
at The Fragrance Foundation**
145 East 32nd Street, 9th Floor
NY 10016
Tel: +1 212 725 2755
www.fragrance.org

DEALERS AND AUCTION HOUSES

Albert Amor
37 Bury Street, St James's,
London SW1Y 6AU
Tel: 020 7930 2444
www.albertamor.co.uk

**American Art
Glass Works Inc**
41 Wooster Street, 1st floor,
New York, NY 10013, USA
Tel: 001 212 625 0783
www.
americanartglassgallery.com

**Andrew Lineham
Fine Glass**
PO Box 465, Chichester,
West Sussex PO18 8WZ.
Tel: 01243 576 241
Mob: 07767 702 722
www.antiquecolouredglass.
info

Arthur Millner
2 Campden Street,
London W8 7EP
Tel: 020 7229 3268
www.arthurmillner.com

Auction Team Köln
Postfach 50 11 19, Bonner
Str. 528-530, D-50971
Cologne, Germany
Tel: 0049 221 38 70 49
www.breker.com

Auktionshaus Bergmann
Möhrendorfestrasse 4
91056 Erlangen, Germany
Tel: 0049 9 131 450 666
www.auction-bergmann.de

Auktionhaus Kaupp
Schloss Sulzburg,
Hauptstrasse 62, 79295
Sulzberg, Germany
Tel: 0049 7634 5038 0
www.kaupp.de

Axtell Antiques
1 River Street, Deposit,
New York 13754 USA
Tel: 001 607 467 2353
www.axtellantiques.com

Block Glass Ltd.
www.blockglass.com

Bloomsbury Auctions
Bloomsbury House,
24 Maddox Street,
London W1 S1PP
Tel: 020 7495 9494
www.bloomsburyauctions.
com

Bonhams, Bond Street
101 New Bond Street,
London W1S 1SR
Tel: 020 7629 6602
www.bonhams.com

Cheffins
Clifton House
1&2 Clifton Road,
Cambridge,
Cambridgeshire CB1 7EA
Tel: 01223 213 343
www.cheffins.co.uk

Chisholm Larsson
145 8th Avenue,

New York, NY 10011, USA
Tel: 001 212 741 1703
www.chisholm-poster.com

Cottees
The Market, East Street,
Wareham, Dorset, BH20 4NR
Tel: 01929 552 826 or
01929 554 915
http://www.
auctionsatcottees.co.uk/

David Rago Auctions
333 North Main Street,
Lambertville, NJ 08530, USA
Tel: 001 609 397 9374
www.ragoarts.com

**David Rago/Nicholas
Dawes Lalique Auctions**
333 North Main Street,
Lambertville,
NJ 08530, USA
Tel: 001 609 397 9374
www.ragoarts.com

Decodame.com
www.decodame.com

Deco Etc
122 West 25th Street
New York, NY 10001, USA
Tel: 001 212 675 3326
www.decoetc.net

The Design Gallery
5 The Green, Westerham,
Kent TN16 1AS
Tel: 01959 561 234
www.designgallery.co.uk

Dreweatt Neate
(Formerly Bracketts)
Tunbridge Wells Saleroom,
The Auction Hall,
The Pantiles, Tunbridge
Wells, Kent TN2 5QL
Tel: 01892 544500
www.dnfa.com/
tunbridgewells
Tel: 01629 574460

Dreweatt Neate
Donnington
Priory Salerooms,
Donnington, Newbury,
Berkshire RG14 2JE
Tel: 01635 553553
www.dnfa.com/donnington

Dreweatt Neate
(Formely Hamptons)
Baverstock House,
93 High Street, Godalming,
Surrey GU7 1AL
Tel: 01483 423 567
www.dnfa.com/godalming

Dreweatt Neate
(Formerly Neales)
The Nottingham Salerooms,
192 Mansfield Road,
Nottingham NG1 3HU
Tel: 0115 962 4141
www.dnfa.com/nottingham

Freeman's
1808 Chestnut Street,
Philadelphia, PA 19103, USA
Tel: 001 215 563 9275
www.freemansauction.com

Galerie Mariska Dirkx
Wilhelminasingel 67,
NL-6041 CH Roermond,
Holland
Tel: 0031 (0)475 317137
www.galeriemariskadirkx.nl

The Glass Merchant
Tel: 07775 683 961

Goodwins Antiques
15 & 16 Queensferry
Street, Edinburgh,
Midlothian EH2 4QW
Tel: 0131 225 4717

Gorringes
15 North Street, Lewes,
East Sussex BN7 2PD
Tel: 01273 472 503
www.gorringes.co.uk

Halcyon Days
14 Brook Street,
London W1S 1BD
Tel: 020 7629 8811
www.halcyondays.co.uk

Herr Auctions
WG Herr Art & Auction
House, Friesenwall 35,
50672 Cologne, Germany
Tel: 00 49 221 25 45 48
www.herr-auktionen.de

Huxtins
PO Box 325, Reedsville,
WV 26547, USA
www.huxtins.com

John Bull (Antiques) Ltd.
JB Silverware,
139A New Bond Street,
London W1S 2TN
Tel: 020 7629 1251
www.antique-silver.co.uk
www.jbsilverware.co.uk

James D Julia Inc
PO Box 830, Fairfield,
ME 04937, USA
Tel: 001 207 453 7125
www.juliaauctions.com

**Kunst-Auktionhaus
Martin Wendl**
August-Bebel-Strasse
4, 07407 Rudolstadt,
Germany
Tel: 0049 3672 4243 50
www.auktionhaus-wendl.de

**Lawrence's
Fine Art Auctioneers**
The Linen Yard, South
Street, Crewkerne,
Somerset TA18 8AB
Tel: 01460 73041
www.lawrences.co.uk

Lyon & Turnbull Ltd.
33 Broughton Place,
Edinburgh,
Midlothian EH1 3RR
Tel: 0131 557 8844
www.lyonandturnbull.com

Linda Bee
Grays Antique Market Mews,
1–7 Davies Street,
London, W1Y 2LP
Tel: 020 7629 5921
www.graysantiques.com

Law Fine Art Ltd.
Ash Cottage, Ashmore
Green, Newbury,
Berkshire, RG18 9ER
Tel: (01635) 860033
www.lawfineart.co.uk

**Mary Wise
& Grosvenor Antiques**
58 Kensington
Church Street,
London W8 4DB
Tel: 020 7937 8649
www.wiseantiques.com

Million Dollar Babies
Tel: 001 518 885 7397

**Otford Antiques and
Collectors Centre**
26–28 High Street,
Otford, Kent TN14 5PQ
Tel: 01959 522 025
www.otfordantiques.co.uk

Pantry and Hearth
994 Main Street South,
Woodbury, CT 06798, USA
Tel: 001 203 263 8555
www.rihada.org/
pantryhearth.htm

Rowley Fine Arts
8 Downham Road,
Ely, Cambridge,
Cambridgeshire CB6 1AH
Tel: 01353 653020
www.rowleyfineart.com

Rumours
4 The Mall
Antiques Arcade,
359 Upper Street,
London, N1 0PD
Tel: 020 7704 6549

The Silver Fund
1 Duke of York Street,
London SW1Y 6JP
Tel: 020 7839 7664
www.thesilverfund.com

Sylvie Spectrum
Stand 372, Grays Antique
Markets, 58 Davies Street,
London W1K 5LP
Tel: 020 7629 3501
spectrum@grays.clara.net

Swann Galleries
104 East 25th Street,
New York, NY 10010, USA

Tel: 001 212 254 4710
www.swanngalleries.com

Sworders
14 Cambridge Road,
Stansted Mountfitchet,
Essex CM24 8BZ
Tel: 01279 817 778
www.sworder.co.uk

Trio
L24 Grays Antique Markets,
58 Davies Street,
London, W1K 5LP
Tel: 020 7493 2736
www.trio-london.fsnet.co.uk

Victoriana Dolls
101 Portobello Rd,
London, W11 2BQ
Tel: 01737 249 525

**William Wain
at Antiquarius**
Stand J6, Antiquarius,
135 King's Road, Chelsea,
London SW3 4PW
Tel: 020 7351 4905

Woolley & Wallis
51–61 Castle St, Salisbury,
Wiltshire SP1 3SU
Tel: 01722 424 500
Fax: 01722 424 508
enquiries@woolleyandwa
llis.co.uk
www.woolleyandwallis.
co.uk

INDEX

PICTURE CREDITS

The following images, photographed with permission from the sources itemized below are copyright © Judith Miller and Dorling Kindersley.

ACKNOWLEDGMENTS

AUTHOR'S ACKNOWLEDGMENTS

The Price Guide Company would like to thank the following for their contribution to the production of this book:

Photographer Graham Rae for his wonderful photography.

All of the dealers, auction houses, and private collectors for kindly allowing us to photograph their collections, especially David Rago, Linda Bee, Nicholas M. Dawes, and Teresa Clayton at Trio.

Also special thanks to Dan Dunlavey, Mark Hill, Sandra Lange, Cathy Marriott, Claire Smith, and Sara Sturgess for their editorial contribution and help with image sourcing.

Thanks also to Digital Image Co-ordinator Ellen Sinclair and Workflow Consultant Bob Bousfield.

PUBLISHER'S ACKNOWLEDGMENTS

Dorling Kindersley would like to thank the following for their contribution to the production of this book:

Sarah Smithies for picture research, Sara Sha'ath for proofreading, Tamsin Curtis for proofreading and co-ordinating proofs, Dawn Henderson and Kathryn Wilkinson for additional editorial help, and Hilary Bird for indexing.